Shadows
and SUBSTANCE

The Truth About Jewish Roots
and Christian Believers

NEIL SILVERBERG

Shadows and Substance: The Truth About Jewish Roots and Christian Believers

Trilogy Christian Publishers
A Wholly Owned Subsidiary of Trinity Broadcasting Network
2442 Michelle Drive Tustin, CA 92780

Rights Department, 2442 Michelle Drive, Tustin, CA 92780.

Trilogy Christian Publishing/TBN and colophon are trademarks of Trinity Broadcasting Network.

Cover design by: Trilogy
Front cover image by: Rudy Bagozzi, www.shutterstock.com
Back cover image by: Javarman, www.shutterstock.com

For information about special discounts for bulk purchases, please contact Trilogy Christian Publishing.

Manufactured in the United States of America
10 9 8 7 6 5 4 3 2 1
Library of Congress Cataloging-in-Publication Data is available.

ISBN: 978-1-63769-650-7
E-ISBN: 978-1-63769-651-4

DEDICATION

I dedicate this work to the churches in *Masterbuilders*
with whom I shared many of these things
and from whom I have learned so much.

A special mention to the leadership team
who saw the value in this book
and continually encouraged me to complete it.

I owe them a debt of love and gratitude.

ACKNOWLEDGMENTS

I want to thank two people whose love and support, not to mention their tireless work on this project, made it possible: Patty King and Grant King. They both took many hours reading the manuscript and helping to get it in its final form. I also want to mention the elder team at Trinity Community Church, who encouraged me to pursue this work when I wanted to give up. Thanks for supporting and believing in me.

And last (but actually first), as I have in all of my other books, a special thanks to my wife, Shelly—a true helpmate that encourages me to pursue all that God calls me to do. Her love, patience, and belief uphold me with strength when I need it most. Thanks for being who you are, Shell.

TABLE OF CONTENTS

ENDORSEMENT

"I've waited years for a book like this to be published. Neil Silverberg has provided for us a thoroughly biblical and pastorally wise evaluation of the Hebrew Roots Movement that I can wholeheartedly endorse. He tethers his conclusions to the Word of God and demonstrates the life-transforming glory of how Jesus Christ is the fulfillment of the Old Testament.

While contending that the HRM is a dangerous trend among many today, he does so with pastoral concern and a love for both the Old Testament and the Jewishness of Jesus. If you've encountered people in the HRM and are confused by their claims, this book is for you."

—Sam Storms, PhD
Bridgeway Church, Oklahoma City, OK

PREFACE

In a certain sense, I have lived with this book for the entirety of my walk with Jesus, the Messiah. Except for a short time after my initial conversion when I was superficially involved with Messianic Judaism, I have spent the majority of my spiritual journey in the Church. I tried to fit into a messianic congregation early in my walk. However, after a dynamic encounter with the Lord, while planting a church in New York City with my brother, God opened my eyes to His intention to create out of both Jew and Gentile "one new man" (Ephesians 2:15). As a result of this experience, I was (as they say in the South) "ruint." I knew God called me to spend the remainder of my days with both Jew and Gentile in the Church, the body of the Messiah.

It was not until many years later, while attempting to help a local church deal with aberrant Hebrew Roots teaching tearing it apart, that I conceived this book. But as often happens, the busyness of life and the pressures of ministry crowded out that initial impression, and the planned book was put on hold. It was actually several years later that I began to put pen to paper (fingers to keyboard).

Like previous works, as I began working on this project, it developed in unexpected ways. Several chapters not in the original plan are now a part of the book. It took a long time to get the manuscript in its present form. Such is the nature of writing books; you start with a general idea but are carried by the wind of the Spirit as the project grows.

Some readers will undoubtedly wish I had spent more time dealing with topics only touched upon superficially. Instead, I chose to focus largely on the core issues defining the Hebrew Roots Movement. Those other issues are important, but to include them would have required a much larger book. For example, I could have said much more about Messianic Judaism in this work but deliberately limited myself to theological matters and practices pertaining to the Hebrew Roots Movement. Besides, there are already excellent works dealing with Messianic Judaism for those readers who are interested.

Throughout the book, I address the theological beliefs of much of the Movement while avoiding attacking people. I respect those who grapple with these things, even though I disagree with much of what they teach. I have quoted many well-known Hebrew Roots Movement teachers not to disparage them but to set forth their theological convictions in the light of what Scripture teaches. One would expect such quotations in a book dealing with a topic like this.

Last of all, I hope the reader understands that I have a deep love for the Lord of glory and the body of the Messiah, where I have lived the entirety of my life. May these words encourage a generation to love the Lord and help perfect a bride as she is adorned for her husband.

— Neil Silverberg,
Knoxville, Tennessee, 2021

INTRODUCTION

The "Hebrew Roots Movement" (hereafter identified as the HRM) is a generic term for a worldwide movement sharing in common two main theological premises. First is the belief that the Christian Church has veered from its original "Jewish" root system and, as a result, has embraced paganism. According to this view, the only way to reconnect to the original root system is to renounce its pagan practices and return to the original faith by practicing such things as the weekly Sabbath and the Jewish Feasts.

The second is the belief that Jesus never abrogated the Law but expected his followers to obey it. Many HRM teachers quote passages such as Matthew 5:17 as the basis for the belief that all believers, both Jew and Gentile, are still under the Law. Beyond that, the movement is widely divergent as to what it practices and believes. These two things remain at the core of what most in the HRM believe.

The HRM differs from Messianic Judaism, which consists largely of Jewish believers who continue living a Jewish lifestyle after becoming believers in Jesus as the Messiah (although there are many non-Jews in most messianic synagogues). The HRM is mostly comprised of Gentiles who have embraced the view that the Church has veered from its original root system and that to live out the faith properly, they must reject the paganism practiced in most Protestant churches and return to biblical faith.

Whenever I've mentioned I was writing a book dealing with the HRM, people have asked why a book like this was necessary. "Aren't there already two books in the New Testament, Galatians and Hebrews, dealing with that topic?" some have asked. While I agree that these two New Testament books address some of the issues raised by the HRM, I still think a book like this is needed. As is the case with other heresies, the HRM have their predetermined answers to these biblical books. People get in the habit of reading them through the lens of their teachers. If for nothing else, it exposes their faulty attempts to explain away the theology of those twin New Testament books.

There is another reason I believe such a book is needed. It exposes much HRM teaching as simply another form of legalism perverting the Gospel of grace. While this book deals specifically with the legalism of the HRM, its message applies to *any* form of legalism resulting from a failure to understand and believe the Gospel. Legalism is the belief that something other than what God has already done through the work of the Jewish Messiah is needed to bring sinful human beings into a relationship with God. In that regard, this book not only deals with the legalism of the HRM, but it also goes a long way in exposing other forms of legalism plaguing the Church today.

Incidentally, the fact that this book deals with legalism explains why it took so many years to write. For the last three decades, I have been enrolled in a life course that can only be described as "Gospel 101"; *nothing less than a total reorientation of life from the perspective of the Gospel of grace.* It combines learning Gospel theology with the application of it to life and ministry. And learning the Gospel of grace has been the best preparation for learning how to spot legalism whenever it raises its ugly head. Just as Secret Service agents study genuine currency until they are so familiar with it they can spot the counterfeit, becoming aware of the truth of the Gospel has only heightened my ability to recognize its distortions. Even though I have had limited time to study all the features of the HRM, growing in my understanding of the biblical Gospel has given me the needed tools for discerning the errors in much of it.

This book was written with two audiences in mind. First, it is written for Christian leaders who are responsible for protecting their flocks. Over the years, I have had the opportunity to talk with many such leaders who have had to deal firsthand with HRM teaching. I have heard the horror stories of the damage it has done to both churches and families. It has solidified my conviction that leaders would benefit from a single volume, which provides both an understanding of the main theological components of much HRM teaching as well as equips leaders to practically know how to deal with it. The two chapters in the last section of the book address them (leaders) directly.

I also have another audience in mind in writing this book— non-Jewish (Gentile) believers who have some idea that the roots of their faith extend back to Judaism and are desirous to learn more about it. This has made them curious about the HRM and its claim to teach the Hebrew roots of the faith. Some have become acquainted with HRM teaching through visiting various websites, while others have attended small home groups where self-appointed HRM teachers have taught it. What they have heard has begun to make sense, and they are beginning to embrace it. My hope is that this book will serve as a guide so as to be better informed as to whether or not to get more deeply involved with it.

As stated previously, this book addresses much of the theology of the movement. The HRM is based on certain theological presuppositions and interpretations of Scripture that must be carefully analyzed if it is to be properly understood. Take, for example, Jesus' words in the Sermon on the Mount referenced earlier; that He did not come to "abolish the Law or the Prophets; I have not come to abolish them but 'to fulfill them" (Matthew 5:17b). Any book attempting to understand the HRM must examine this vital statement since much of its theology is derived from it. But this book isn't limited to grasping the theology of the movement but addresses a whole host of practical issues as well. Nevertheless, understanding the theology which fuels the movement is critical to being adequately prepared to deal practically with HRM teachers and teaching. That is why so much of this book is theological in nature.

I have arranged the material in this book into five sections, each dealing with a key issue regarding the HRM. First, there are two chapters preceding these five sections foundational to understanding the HRM. The first chapter, "Understanding the Hebrew Roots Movement," provides a brief overview of what the HRM is. This is followed by a chapter entitled "The Hebrews Roots of the Early Church." Not everything the HRM teaches is dangerous; after all, the roots of Christianity *are* deeply imbedded in Judaism. This chapter describes five things the Church should learn by understanding the Hebraic roots of our faith.

The five chapters in Section 1, "The Churches of the Gentiles," examine what first-century apostles taught Gentile believers when it comes to Jewish beliefs and practices. This section includes a chapter dealing with the outcome of the Jerusalem Conference in Acts as well as one addressing the changes Emperor Constantine implemented when he took the throne of the Roman Empire. This chapter challenges the common view taught by many in the HRM that the churches of the first three centuries were essentially Hebraic in belief and practice until Constantine took the throne and extricated the Church from its Hebrew root system. While there is some truth to that, it has been grossly exaggerated. Then there is a chapter dealing with the Sabbath and the HRM teaching that Gentiles are under obligation to observe it. This is followed by a chapter addressing whether believers should observe the Jewish Feasts rather than the Christian holidays (Christmas and Easter). That section concludes with a chapter dealing with Paul's letter to the Philippians. I included it because it is probably the only letter written to a mostly Gentile congregation. As such, it gives us a firsthand look at what the apostle Paul expected Gentile believers to observe when it comes to Jewish practices.

Section 2, "Jesus the Jew," deals with the Jewishness of Jesus and what it means for Gentile churches. It includes a chapter regarding Paul and the claim of many in the HRM that he invented the religion of Christianity. The two chapters in Section 3, "Hebraic Roots or Jewish Roots?" deals with the difference between the Hebraic roots of the faith derived from the Hebrew Bible and Jewish roots derived from Rabbinic Judaism and Jewish tradition. Many in the HRM fail to distinguish between them, calling people to rabbinic belief and practice rather than biblical Hebraism.

Section 4, entitled "The Key that Unlocks the Door," deals with the importance of interpreting the Old Testament in the light of the revelation given to the apostles in the New. Last but not least, the two chapters in Section 5, entitled "Protecting the Flock," were written with leaders in mind, primarily those with teaching responsibilities in local churches. They deal largely with how leaders should be proactive in protecting their flocks from unbiblical Hebrew roots teaching.

This book will not be appreciated unless the reader understands my zeal to ensure that the Gospel of the grace of God is protected from distortion. I believe that many in the HRM, under the guise of discovering their Hebrew roots, are "deserting him who called you in the grace of Christ and are turning to a different gospel" (Galatians 1:6b). Paul doesn't view the Galatians' embrace of Judaism as a boon to their spiritual development, but desertion of the God who called them by His grace. While many in the HRM believe they have discovered the true roots of their faith, in actuality, they have gone back under the Law. I pray that this book will be used by God to reclaim a new generation of those who are strangers to the Gospel of grace. I long for all who read these pages to grow in love for the Messiah, the Lord Jesus Christ, and for the Gospel of the grace of God. To Him, be the glory forever.

CHAPTER 1

Understanding the Hebrew Roots Movement

The pressure in the room was palpable as I entered the sanctuary. My heart beat nervously as I made my way in and began cordially greeting those who were there. I tried to be cool and collected, but I struggled inwardly. *Why had I consented to participate in this debate in the first place? What was I going to say that would be meaningful and convincing?* My mind thought of all the reasons I was the wrong person for this task. But it was too late; I had accepted the challenge, and the debate was about to begin. Silently, I whispered a prayer to God to help me with the task at hand.

As I walked through the room, I noticed most of the men assembled wore the traditional keepaw (head covering) Orthodox male Jews wear as well as most male Jews when worshipping in the synagogue. Some also had donned the traditional *tallit*, the Jewish prayer shawl male Jews wear when praying. From all appearances, it looked like the beginning of an Orthodox Jewish synagogue service. But it wasn't a synagogue we entered but a church. And these weren't Orthodox Jews assembled but non-Jews (Gentiles), part of the HRM. They believed that the Christian faith has been radically extricated from its original root system in Judaism and that God was calling them to rediscover it. That meant practicing such things as the weekly Sabbath (Saturday), keeping the Jewish feast days, and in some cases, even keeping the dietary laws of the Old Testament.

A pastor friend of mine whose church had been ravaged by HRM teachers invited me to debate some of these teachers in a two-day open forum. This teaching had ripped this church apart, and the pastor was hoping my coming would protect those who remained in the church. So he arranged for several of these teachers to come and debate me with church members present.

This was not my first invitation to this church to address this issue. I actually came some years prior when the church first began to deal with these things. At that time, I preached from the book of Hebrews (I don't know why I am strangely attracted to this book), sounding out the writer of Hebrews' theme that the Law was a mere *shadow* of the good things that came when the Messiah appeared (Hebrews 10:1). I pleaded with those present to lay aside the shadows and embrace the substance which came in Christ. I felt, at that time, like my words really connected with the people.

Nevertheless, the church continued to be ravaged by this teaching, and now I returned to debate these teachers. This time the format was different. Each one would first present his views, followed by questions from the other presenters. Thankfully, I spoke first. I remember a strong sense of the power of God upon me as I spoke. The only other time I experienced such a rich sense of the Spirit's power occurred when I debated two witches, a Satanist, a pantheist, and a religious studies professor on the campus of the University of Tennessee. Interestingly, at that time, I also remember sensing the same measure of weakness going into that debate that I now felt. Perhaps there is something to what Paul said about personal weakness being the basis for divine empowerment (2 Corinthians 12:10).

When I finished speaking, the HRM teachers peppered me with questions. The questioners seemed tolerant at first, but their tone quickly changed to belligerence and, before long, outright disdain. I brought two elders from our local church for support. As one of the elders remembered it, there were times when there was concern that things might even turn physical. Here is how he remembered it:

> When we arrived, it was obvious the leadership of the church was very nervous. There had been a fracture within the church created by those who wanted to follow certain aspects of the Law of Moses and keep Jewish traditions such as the feasts and Sabbath. The problem came when those who wanted to be involved in these activities began to demand that others who didn't feel the same way participate as well. If they refused, then they would be looked at as second-class believers, if at all.
>
> As I recall, when Neil began to minister, he started with the things to which they generally agreed. Believers cannot deny the reality of the rich history found in the Old Testament. He went on to say that it's not even wrong to appreciate the traditions and choose to keep some of them as a personal conviction. Everyone at this point was fairly docile and agreeable to what he said. Neil began at this point to talk about the work of Jesus and how He fulfilled the law. For believers to come under the law once again means Jesus did not finish the work; they conclude His work is incomplete.
>
> The people began to grow palpably restless. At the end of his talk, Neil asked for questions,

and that is when the unrest became evident. There
were challenges made and speeches given to try
to counteract the things that Neil had shared. I
was even frightened at times that there might be
an attempt to harm him physically. He handled
it all with grace while also refusing to back down
from the truth. I'm not certain how things ended
up within the church in the days following this
encounter, but I walked away asking God to always
keep me from falling into such a strong delusion.

— Tyler Lynde,
Senior Elder, Trinity Community Church

The details of those two days, for the most part, remain a blur.
The two elders who accompanied me said I powerfully defended
the Gospel against every assault they could mount. They felt as
if they had been transported back two thousand years and sat
in on one of Paul's synagogue sessions when he defended the
Gospel before a Jewish audience. The whole thing was surreal.
Here I was, the only one in the room actually Jewish, maligned
by Gentiles for failing to live as a Jew after believing.

I doubt I convinced any of those present to return to the
biblical Gospel over those two days. But one thing clearly
emerged from the debate—the conviction that I needed to write
the book you are now reading. I first conceived of this book after
my first visit to the church years before. But now, after these two
days of debate, I knew God was *calling* me to write it

What Exactly Is the HRM?

As I stated in the Introduction, the term "Hebrew Roots"
(sometimes referred to as "Jewish Roots") covers a wide array

of teaching. Yet, there are a couple of key ideas that most HRM teaching shares in common.

The first is the belief that the Church veered from its original Jewish root system and, in the process, adopted pagan beliefs and practices. The website GotQuestions defines it this way:

> The premise of the Hebrew Roots movement is the belief that the Church has veered far from the true teachings and Hebrew concepts of the Bible. The movement maintains that Christianity has been indoctrinated with the culture and beliefs of Greek and Roman philosophy and that ultimately biblical Christianity, taught in churches today, has been corrupted with a pagan imitation of the New Testament Gospels.[1]

Along with the belief that the Church has been influenced by paganism is the belief that Jesus never intended his followers (including Gentiles) to stop leading Torah-observant lives, including seventh-day Sabbath observance and the Jewish Feasts days. On the contrary, they believe that Yeshua (Jesus' Hebrew name, which most of the HRM uses instead of Jesus) came to empower believers to keep it:

> Those of the Hebrew Roots belief hold to the teaching that Christ's death on the cross did not end the Mosaic Covenant but instead renewed it, expanded its message, and wrote it on the hearts of His true followers. They teach that the understanding of the New Testament can only come from a Hebrew perspective and that the teachings of the Apostle Paul are not understood clearly or

taught correctly by Christian pastors today. Many affirm the existence of an original Hebrew-language New Testament and, in some cases, denigrate the existing New Testament text written in Greek. This becomes a subtle attack on the reliability of the text of our Bible. If the Greek text is unreliable and has been corrupted, as charged by some, the Church no longer has a standard of truth.[2]

(All grammar and spelling has been left unedited.)

Summing it up, the HRM is essentially a "response-movement" calling people back to the original Hebrew roots of the faith, which were (supposedly) lost when the Church veered from its original stock. As the article previously stated, even the Greek text of the Bible can't be trusted since it departed from the original Hebrew text. From there, the movement is widely divergent in its practices, running the entire gamut from Sabbath-keeping, observing of the Feasts, and keeping the dietary laws to wearing of keepaws and tallit (head covering and prayer shawl). Most in the HRM share the belief that the coming of the Messiah and His atoning death did not do away with the Mosaic covenant. True believers should, therefore, keep the Law as a demonstration of their love for God. In other words, they should live as Jews.

But has God called Gentile believers to become, in effect, practicing Jews? As I seek to make clear in this book, I don't think so. I will make the case throughout this work that believing Gentiles, alongside their Jewish counterparts who believe, are called to live in and express the "one new man" created by God through the death and resurrection of the Messiah (Ephesians 2:15). That is not to say that Gentile believers have now become physically Jewish or, for that matter, Jews are now physically non-Jewish. Just as men who believe remain men and women remain women, so the distinction outwardly between Jew and Gentile still exists. But what Paul says in the Ephesian letter is true identity is no longer found in anything outward but in that new humanity created by God through the work of His Son.

The Story of Ralph

Ralph (not his real name) was a member of a church where I served as a teaching pastor for several years. He and his family faithfully attended our church until they started going to a Bible study in our area, where they began learning about the Hebrew roots of the faith. Soon after attending the Bible study, Ralph and his family began to pull away from our church, attending sporadically at best. The pastor of our church asked me to check up on them. So I called Ralph and arranged to meet him and his wife later that week at a local restaurant.

When the time came, I met Ralph alone, his wife unable to come. After exchanging pleasantries, I asked him what he was learning in his new Bible study. Ralph conveyed how a whole new world opened up to him through the realization that the true roots of the Christian faith were in Judaism rather than the Roman paganism much of the Church world practiced. He spoke of the enrichment his family had received by observing the Jewish feasts instead of the Christian holidays and keeping the weekly Saturday Sabbath. He believed God was blessing his family for practicing a pure faith, untainted by paganism. Ralph concluded by saying that, based on this new knowledge, he could never go back to normative Christianity.

I listened intently, and when Ralph finished speaking, I responded. I told him I was glad for his newfound discovery of the Hebrew Bible (Old Testament) as the root from which the flower of Christianity blossomed. I agreed with him that having a good foundation in the Old Testament was critical to understanding the New Testament. But then I told him he had overlooked the most fundamental truth: that the Jewish Feasts (as well as other aspects of the Old Testament) were mere shadows which had come in the Messiah and not the very form of these realities (Hebrews 10:1). Since reality has now come in Jesus, there was no longer a need to cling to the shadows. These things could certainly be studied as a means of better understanding the Gospel. Nevertheless, they remain merely shadows. I told him that this is where his Old Testament learning should have brought him, to a heightened understanding of all that has come in the New Covenant.

Ralph listened respectfully, and when I finished, he thanked me for my concern but said he couldn't deny the things he learned. Before I left, I warned him that if he continued on his present course, he and his family would eventually stop attending church altogether. He assured me this would never happen and thanked me for meeting with him. After he left, I remained at the restaurant for a while. I wondered what impact, if any at all, my words made. My mind thought of all the things I should have said while talking with Ralph. Leaving the restaurant, I prayed for him and his family as I drove home. (Incidentally, that was the last time I ever saw Ralph and his family. After our meeting, he stopped coming to church altogether. Later, we heard he was gathering in a home on the Sabbath with other believers who embraced the same teaching. Talk about a self-fulfilling prophecy).

What's strange about this whole episode is that my pastor and I are both Jewish by birth, while Ralph is a Gentile. Could anything be more ironic? Two Jews pleaded with a non-Jewish man not to practice Judaism, while he frowned on us for living like Gentiles.

Why Such a Blessing?

Ralph is just one example of the thousands of Gentile believers in Jesus who testify of the life-transforming blessings they have received by returning to the Hebrew roots of their faith. Many of these believers speak of discovering a richness they had not previously known while practicing traditional Christianity. Why do so many non-Jewish believers testify to such a heightened sense of blessing when embracing the HRM?

I believe there are a couple of reasons that account for this. As previously mentioned, the discovery of the richness of the Old Testament as the sourcebook for New Testament theology and practice is certainly one of them. Considering that most non-Jewish believers today are not taught the Hebrew Scriptures in any significant way, this is not difficult to understand. Once exposed to the richness of the Hebrew Bible as the foundation for all they have come to know and love in the New Testament, it makes sense that they receive a heightened sense of blessing. I have personally witnessed this when teaching the Old Testament to Gentile believers in the churches where I have served. It is as if these believers have discovered a whole new world. And they have—the world of the Hebrew Bible. So it should not be surprising that they testify of such blessing.

Yet, there is another reason that may account for the heightened sense of blessing. Embracing the HRM has allowed non-Jews to relate to the nation of Israel in a totally new way. Instead of reading the Old Testament as a history book of an ancient people, they have begun reading it as a book detailing the rich history of a covenant people, whose history they now fully share (Ephesians 2:11-13, 3:6). And this new identification creates a love for the Jewish people and the nation of Israel, which is a positive force when sharing the Gospel with Jews. Many Jews are persuaded that most Gentiles hate them. When they meet instead with love, compassion, and a deep appreciation for Israel from Gentiles, it is a powerful means of convincing them of the truth of the Gospel. The apostle Paul seems to allude to this when speaking of God's mysterious plan to provoke Jews to jealousy through the mercy he has shown to non-Jews (see Romans 11:13-14).

There is also a third reason which may account for the sense of blessedness many Gentile believers experience embracing the Jewish roots of their faith. I deal with it much later in this book. It is the mistaken belief that it is infinitely better to be a "Jewish" believer than a "non-Jewish" believer. Since "non-Jewish" believers cannot change birth, they are robbed of this blessing. But now, through Jewish Roots teaching, many Gentiles are being taught that by practicing a Jewish lifestyle, they have, in fact, become Jewish.

Yet the truth is, Gentile believers *should* rejoice in the blessedness of joining Israel, not because they practice the Jewish feasts and keep the Sabbath, but as a result of the salvation work of the Messiah. What could be more blessed than that? Previously, they were

> at that time separated from Christ, alienated from the commonwealth of Israel and strangers to the covenants of promise, having no hope and without God in the world. But now in Christ Jesus, you who once were *p*far off have been brought near *q*by the blood of Christ,
>
> — Ephesians 2:12-13

This is the result of the Messiah's redeeming work, not because Gentiles are keeping the Law. They are blessed because they are *in* Christ.

Hebrew Roots Movement Versus
Messianic Judaism

This book is focused primarily on understanding the HRM and its beliefs regarding non-Jewish believers. That being the case, it does not directly address Messianic Judaism or Messianic Jewish congregations.

In my early years as a believer, I was loosely involved with Messianic Jewish congregations. One of the largest Messianic congregations in the country met in the neighborhood where I grew up. The Messianic rabbi of that congregation performed the ceremony at our wedding. Messianic Jewish congregations are congregations of (largely) Jewish believers who, after becoming believers in Yeshua as the Messiah, desire to live Jewish lifestyles. These congregations meet on the Sabbath, celebrate the feasts, and raise their children as Jews who are believers (as opposed to being Christians). The rationale for these congregations is that Jews won't enter a church and must hear the Gospel in a Jewish context.

In an attempt to underscore that Jews can believe in Jesus without ceasing to be Jewish, many messianic congregations became known as messianic *synagogues*, their services mimicking typical Jewish synagogue services complete with Torah and Haftorah readings and kissing the ark as it passes through the congregation. By referring to themselves as synagogues rather than congregations, it is a further step away from identifying themselves as part of the Church, a step deemed necessary to underscore they are Jews rather than Christians. Messianic synagogues now exist in most major American cities and are represented by at least two major messianic denominations.

Is there a difference between the HRM and messianic Jewish synagogues? There is, though they do share a lot in common. While both believe that God is restoring the original faith, which was lost, Messianic Judaism is largely a movement among Jews who have come to believe in Yeshua. It is not difficult to understand why many Jews would want to continue practicing some semblance of Jewish faith and identity after coming to believe in Jesus as the Messiah, especially those who formerly were practicing Jews. While many Gentiles attend messianic synagogues, the appeal to Gentiles is downplayed in messianic synagogues.

But it is exactly the opposite when it comes to the HRM. The basic appeal is to Gentiles, seeking to persuade them that the Gentile Christianity they practice is rooted in paganism and that only by returning to the Hebrew roots of the faith can they ever hope to be faithful to God. That is why the majority of HRM devotees today are Gentiles.

British Israelism

There is another form of the HRM that is not addressed directly in this book, technically known as British Israelism or Anglo-Israelism. This is the "belief that the people of the British Isles are 'genetically, racially, and linguistically the direct descendants of the ten lost tribes of ancient Israel.'"[3] According to the doctrine, the ten lost tribes of Israel found their way to Western Europe and Britain, becoming the ancestors of the British and related peoples. And since the United States was peopled by the British Isles, Americans (according to this view) are descendants of the ten lost tribes. According to this view, this accounts for the blessedness that has rested on this country. In the latter part of the twentieth century, Herbert T. Armstrong was a strong proponent of this doctrine.

Not only can this doctrine not be historically upheld, in the end, it makes very little difference in our spiritual lives. I once spoke to a man who believed and defended it vigorously. When he finished speaking, I asked him one simple question, "So what?" What I meant by the question was what difference did it make if it was true since Jesus said the "flesh profits nothing" (John 6:63). If it can be proven that the Brittany people are the Ten Lost Tribes of Israel, what difference did it make in the long run? Still, people who hold to this doctrine defend it to the death, treating it as the most important doctrine in Scripture. Like other forms of error, they put their faith completely in what can only be described as conjecture instead of the solid truth of God's word.

What Lies Ahead?

In this chapter, we focused on gaining a good overview of what the HRM is. At best, we just did a quick flyover without really landing the plane. Still, it was necessary to gain an overall understanding of the core identity defining the HRM.

Before looking at what the first-century apostles taught Gentiles to observe, I have inserted a chapter I hope will safeguard against the misunderstanding that there is nothing the Church can learn from its connection to our Hebrew roots. On the contrary, the Church certainly gains much from its connection to its Hebrew root system. As New Testament believers, the roots of our faith *are* Hebraic, stretching back to the faith of the Hebrew Bible (Old Testament) and the rich history of Israel. In the next chapter, I identify five specific things the Church gleans from her connection to its Hebrew root system.

CHAPTER 2

Hebrew Roots
of the Early Church

In the last chapter, we looked briefly at the HRM as a movement claiming to restore the true roots of the Christian faith. This movement is attracting thousands of non-Jews (Gentiles) worldwide, promising them restoration to the true faith as taught by Jesus and the apostles. It teaches Gentiles that the true roots of their faith are in Judaism rather than the paganism practiced in much of the modern Church today.

Like many forms of error, the HRM contains a mixture of biblical truth with unbiblical notions rooted in human tradition. In this chapter, we will examine the biblical truth we can learn from discovering the Hebrew roots of the faith. Not everything taught in the HRM is bad. Since the HRM teaches that the Church is sustained by a Hebrew root system, it highlights an important truth. It reminds us that the Church emerged out of the womb of the faith of the Old Testament.

Sadly, much of the modern Church is ignorant of this truth. There is a great need, therefore, to help believers understand the Hebrew roots of their faith. But as I hope to demonstrate throughout this book, there is a profound difference between learning the Hebraic roots of the faith derived from the Hebrew Bible and those things derived from Rabbinic Judaism and

Jewish tradition. Many HRM teachers today teach Gentiles to observe things taught in Rabbinic Judaism and Jewish tradition rather than those learned from the Hebrew Bible. We don't read anything in Scripture about wearing skull caps or prayer shawls as the way to becoming more Jewish. But in learning the true roots of our faith derived from the Hebrew Bible, we learn much about our *true* Hebraic roots.

What things can we learn from understanding the Hebrew roots of our faith derived from the Hebrew Bible? In this chapter, we focus on five central components of the roots of our faith. They are: understanding the Hebrew Scriptures as the sourcebook for all the New Testament teaches; an understanding of the Person of God; an understanding of the people of God; a covenantal celebration (the Lord's Supper) and God's people as a people called to be separate from the world.

The Wonderful Hebrew Bible

When asking the twin questions in the Roman letter, "What advantage has the Jew? Or what is the value of circumcision?" Paul refers to the fact that the Jewish people were "entrusted with the oracles of God" (Romans 3:1-2). This is a reference primarily to the giving of the Law at Mount Sinai. Almost a million Jews stood and heard the voice of the living God speaking the "Ten Commandments" (Exodus 34:28b). No other nation ever heard the voice of the living God speaking from the midst of the fire and lived (Deuteronomy 5:4). As Stephen reminded the Sanhedrin, Moses "is the one who was in the congregation in the wilderness with the angel who spoke to him at Mount Sinai, and with our fathers. He received living oracles to give to us" (Acts 7:38).

Furthermore, it was Jews who painstakingly stewarded each word they received, carefully writing them down for future

generations. Sadly, very few in the Church today understand the
debt of love owed the Jewish people for painstakingly preserving
Holy Scripture. An anonymous poem entitled "The Jew" not
only reflects on this privilege given to the Jewish people, but
it also underscores the Church's need to pray for the seed of
Abraham continually:

> Scattered by God's almighty hand,
> Afflicted and forlorn,
> Sad wanderers from their pleasant Land,
> Do Judah's children mourn;
> And even in Christian countries, few
> Breathe thoughts of pity for the Jew.

> Yet listen, Gentile, do you love
> The Bible's precious page?
> Then let your heart with kindness move
> To Israel's heritage;
> Who traced those lines of love for you?
> Each sacred writer was a Jew.

> And then as years and ages passed,
> And Nations rose and fell,
> Though clouds and darkness oft were cast
> O'er captive Israel
> The oracles of God for you
> Were kept in safety by the Jew.

> And when the great Redeemer came
> For guilty man to bleed.
> He did not take an angel's name,
> No, born of Abraham's seed,

Jesus, who gave His life for you—
The gentle Saviour—was a Jew.

And though His own received Him not,
And turned in pride away,
Whence is the Gentile's happier lot?
Are you more just than they?
No! God in pity turned to you—
Have you no pity for the Jew?

Go, then, and bend your knee to pray
For Israel's ancient race;
Ask the dear Saviour every day
To call them by His grace.
Go, for a debt of love is due
From Christian Gentiles to the Jew.

Author unknown

Paul refers to the entire Old Testament as the "Prophetic Writings" (Romans 16:26), while the Church refers to it as "God's Word *Written*" (in juxtaposition to "God's Word *Person*"). He also describes these writings as "God-breathed" (2 Timothy 3:16). While this includes the New Testament, it primarily refers to the Hebrew Bible, the Old Testament (the New Testament not yet completed when Paul wrote these words).

The Jewish people recognized three divisions of the Holy Scripture as opposed to the four divisions of the Church. They are *Torah* (five books of Moses), *Prophets* (which includes the historical books of Samuel and Kings), and *Writings* (sometimes called the Psalms, being the largest book in that division). In the English Bible, the Old Testament is comprised of 39 books, while the Hebrew Bible has only 22 (based on the fact that there are twenty-two letters in the Hebrew alphabet). Why the difference? All of the same material in the English Old Testament is in the Hebrew Old Testament, only it is arranged differently. As previously stated, there are no books of 1 and 2 Samuel or 1 and 2 Kings but simply the book of Samuel, Kings, and Chronicles in the Hebrew Bible. So while there are fewer books, all of the material in the English Old Testament found in the thirty-nine books are in the Hebrew version as well. In Luke's account of the appearance of the resurrected Messiah to the apostles in the Upper Room (Luke 24:44), Jesus recognized the three divisions of the Hebrew Bible:

> "These are my words that I spoke to you while I was still with you, that everything written about me in the *Law of Moses* and the *Prophets* and the *Psalms* must be fulfilled." Then He opened their minds to understand the Scriptures.
>
> — Luke 24: 44-45 (italics mine)

The phrase "He opened their minds to understand the Scriptures" does not mean He introduced them for the first time to their Hebrew Bible. It can't mean that since, as Jews, they were thoroughly acquainted with Scripture from birth. Rather, it meant He painstakingly took them through each division, showing how He was the key that unlocked it all. What must it have been like to have the resurrected Messiah Himself take them through each section of the Hebrew Bible, showing how it all pointed to Him! We don't have to wonder since the two on the road to Emmaus left us a report of what they experienced as the risen Messiah opened up the Scriptures to them, "They said to each other, 'Did not our hearts *burn* within us while he talked to us on the road, while he opened to us the Scriptures'" (Luke 24:32; italics mine).

For the Church, the Hebrew Bible is the foundation of the apostolic teaching found in the New Testament. While that includes quotations from the Old Testament, it also means that the rich contours of Hebrew thought formed the basis of New Testament theology. G.A.F. Knight has observed that "If God chose Israel, then he also chose to use the Hebrew language. If we accept the obvious fact, we must proceed to accept more. The Hebrews had their own peculiar manner of thinking about most things in heaven and earth." [1]

Wilson goes on to say that "because they were an intimate part of the religious world of Israel, they reflected, primarily and fundamentally, a Hebraic way of looking at life." [2] While there is evidence Paul also drew some from the Hellenistic Western world in his teaching, it is clear that the Hebrew Bible and Hebrew thought formed the basis of *most* of the theological content of his teaching.

During his earthly ministry, Jesus made constant reference to the Hebrew Bible because, for him, it remained the final authority for faith and practice. When his disciples were accused of eating the heads of grain on the Sabbath, Jesus quoted an episode from the life of David, which settled the matter (Matthew 12:1-5). When asked by the Pharisees for a sign, he told them there would be no sign given except that of the sign of Jonah (Matthew 12:38-41). The Queen of the South would sit in judgment on his generation because she came from the ends of the earth to hear the wisdom of Solomon, and Someone greater than Solomon was here (Matthew 12:41). We have already referred to the fact that after rising from the dead, Jesus took the apostles through each division of the Hebrew Bible, demonstrating how each one referred to Him (Luke 24:44-45). Before His death, Jesus quoted several portions of Scripture to defend His action, thus demonstrating He held the Hebrew Scriptures to be the ultimate authority in questions of faith and practice for the people of God.

The same is true in the apostle Paul's writings. He refers to the three divisions of the Hebrew Bible as "breathed out by God and profitable for teaching, reproof, correction, and training in righteousness" (2 Timothy 3:16). In a word, the entire Old Testament was the sourcebook of all the Church believed. Later, when the New Testament writings were completed, they were added to the Old Testament to complete the canon.

Down through the centuries, several attempts were made to sever the New Testament from its Old Testament roots. Marcion, a second-century heretic, reformatted the entire canon of Scripture, excluding the Old Testament as well as the Gospels (except for portions of Luke). He rejected the idea that the God of the Old Testament and the God of the New was the same. For Marcion, the God of the Old Testament was inferior to the New. Marcion's canon only included ten of the writings of the apostle Paul who was his favorite apostle. But even Paul's writings were not exempt from being excised—he cut out any reference to Judaism even in the great apostle's letters. The mention of Abraham as an example of faith was eliminated from Galatians (Galatians 3:6-9) as well as the connection between the law and the Gospels (Galatians 3:15-25). The Church eventually rejected Marcion for his heretical views and maintained the Old Testament as the foundation for all of the New Testament beliefs.

While the majority of the Church today would agree with Marcion's condemnation, many believers today only give lip service to the Old Testament. While recognizing that the Old Testament contains prophecies of the coming Messiah as well as important moral instruction, there is very little understanding that Hebrew thought, as well as the uniqueness of the Hebrew language, formed the basis of much New Testament theology. While we may not be followers of Marcion, we subtly have become Neo-Marcion in our attitude toward the Old Testament:

> Nevertheless, in our concerted effort to be "New Testament" believers, we have too often unconsciously minimized the place and importance of the Old Testament and the Church's Hebraic roots. At worst, many so-called Bible-believing Christians have become de facto "quarter-of-the-Bible" adherents (the New Testament has 260 chapters to the Old Testament's 929 chapters); at best, they rely on a "loose-leaf" edition of the Old Testament.[3]

An example of that is the continued attempts to understand the book of Revelation apart from the Old Testament. Few seem to realize that every verse in Revelation is either an echo or else a direct quote from the Old Testament. Little wonder, therefore, that people go to the Wall Street Journal or USA Today to find its meaning rather than the pages of the Hebrew Bible.

Salvation Is of the Jews

When Jesus uttered the words "salvation is of the Jews" to a Samaritan woman, he was not declaring God was only interested in saving Jews (John 4:22). Rather, he reminded her God revealed Himself and his plan to save sinners first to the Jewish people. Among other things, that means the human race is dependent on the Jew for its concept of God.

In theology, there is often a distinction made between *general* revelation and *special* revelation. General revelation is that which

God gives to all peoples of the earth. It is general because people gain revelation through observing the things God has made, which everyone has access to (Romans 1:19-20). But the revelation God gave to the Jewish people falls into the category of *special* revelation in that God made it known to them in a special way. Once Israel received it, they wrote it down for other generations to read and study. Thus, the Old Testament (as well as the New when added later) contains a special revelation of God, which Israel stewarded for the nations.

Therefore, to know God, it is first necessary to grapple with the revelation of God given to Israel and contained in Holy Scripture. It is through their history, culture, and language that the whole matter of salvation is understood. Simply stated, salvation is a Hebrew thing. But it is not only the Hebrew people and their language and culture God used to communicate to the human race who he is and what he has done. Paul's letters indicate he occasionally drew from the Hellenistic world as well. Still, the evidence seems conclusive that the Hebraic rather than Hellenistic world was the source of much of his theology:

> But one must certainly recognize that Paul used
> Greek to aid communication (e.g., his extensive
> use of the Septuagint, the Greek translation of the
> Old Testament), and he employed certain stylistic
> devices (Greek historical forms and phrases) so as
> to present material in a manner the audience would
> understand. But some claim that discontinuity
> extends to the sources of Paul's religious thought
> in pagan Hellenistic beliefs. However, scholars
> have marshaled considerable material to oppose
> the popular position that early Christianity was a

syncretistic faith which borrowed its essential beliefs from Hellenistic philosophy or religion.[4]

What Jesus made clear to the Samaritan woman is that the Jew carefully preserved the knowledge of the true and living God. That revelation was not the result of syncretistic development but was given to Israel when God made Himself known to their fathers, Abraham, Isaac, and Jacob. God carefully preserved that revelation until He revealed Himself to the entire nation at Mount Sinai.

A People for His Name

It is vital to remember that God gave this revelation to the *people* of Israel, not merely individuals. At Sinai, He told Israel they would be His "treasured possession among all the peoples, for all the earth is mine" (Exodus 19:5b). This produced in the nation a corporate consciousness eventually passed on to the Church. In a word, Israel thought of itself as a "redeemed" community.

It is not surprising, therefore, that no prayers in Judaism ever begin with the word "I," but always with "our" or "we." Jews were taught that God saved a people out of Egypt, not merely individuals. Jesus Himself, emerging as He did out of the rich contours of the Hebrew religion, taught His disciples to pray with the same corporate consciousness ("*Our* Father, in heaven"). This was the mindset of the Hebrew people, and it was passed on to the Church since the first believers were all Jews. Luke's description of that first believing community in Acts is a clear depiction of the communal nature of the people of God (Acts 2:41-47).

The Jewish community continues to model for the Church how to live out her faith in the context of community. Despite pressures to assimilate, the Jewish people to this day exist as a separate community. While this may be attributed to their need for survival, it is more likely the result of having been birthed as a "covenant" community. From the moment of their adoption at Sinai, this consciousness of being a redeemed people was ingrained in their thinking. Even though only one generation stood at the mountain and heard God audibly speak the ten words, Moses reminds them that every Israelite stood at Sinai and heard the voice of God (Deuteronomy 5:1-5).

This corporate consciousness, kept alive in the Church as it remained in the East, began to diminish as the Gospel moved westward. There it encountered Hellenism with its primary focus on the individual as opposed to the community. Church life became more about the spiritual benefits individuals receive rather than living out the faith within the context of a community. Sadly, for millions of Western believers today, Church continues to be a place one attends rather than a community to whom one belongs.

In this regard, we can learn much from the Jewish community. We in the West desperately need to return to an understanding of Church as a community. Nothing can substitute for transparent relationships where people encounter each other outside of church meetings. This is not to downplay the importance of church gatherings but simply to sound out the reminder that believers are called to true community. As important as church meetings are, church life was intended to be radically more than several hundred strangers singing songs and listening to a sermon. We must be a people led by the Gospel into the sharing of our lives in transparency and commitment.

Passover and the Lord's Supper

When the Lord delivered His people from Egyptian bondage and brought them to a mountain, He told them that His Lordship would be reflected in their lives by the manner in which they arranged their annual calendar. During certain times of the year, they were to celebrate various feasts to the Lord (Exodus 23:14-17). The first of these, Passover, fell in the spring and was the beginning of the year for them since it celebrated their redemption as a people (Exodus 12:1-2). God wanted them to start their year thinking of themselves as a redeemed people.

Passover was celebrated by the sharing of a special meal on the night of the fourteenth of the month of Nisan. Later in Jewish history, this meal became known as the Seder. After the lamb was slaughtered and its blood applied to the mantel and lintel of the door, it was eaten with unleavened bread and bitter herbs (Exodus 12:7-11). Whatever was not eaten was to be consumed with fire; nothing was to be left till morning (Exodus 12:8-10). Fire typifies divine judgment, thus foreshadowing the Lamb of God who would one day consume, in his own person, the wrath due us all.

Later in Jewish history, the Seder took on additional customs, such as the drinking of four cups of wine intermittently throughout the evening. This custom probably had its origins during the Babylonian Captivity when Israel, banished from their homeland, had no temple to sacrifice their lambs. One reason cups of wine are used may be due to the fact that the Lord is portrayed throughout the Hebrew Bible as holding in his hand a cup of judgment which he pours out on the earth (Psalm 75:8). The cup, therefore, clearly illustrates divine wrath.

This symbol of a cup of divine wrath is carried over in the New Testament as well. On the night He was betrayed, Jesus referred to drinking the cup His Father gave Him twice in the Garden of Gethsemane. First, Jesus asked the Father to remove the cup from Him (Luke 22:42). It is unlikely that He was shrinking back primarily from the physical pain He was about to experience but was beginning to bear in His own Person the full measure of the wrath of God against sinners. The second reference to a cup came in response to Peter cutting off the high priest's servant's ear. Jesus told him, "Put your sword into its sheath; shall I not drink the cup that the Father has given me?" (John 18:11). In both instances, the focus was on the judgment He would take upon Himself to accomplish human redemption. There is no other way human beings could be redeemed than by the Son of God drinking the cup of the wrath of God fully.

But if a cup represents the wrath of God, it also is a symbol of redemption. Piecing together the events in the Upper Room on the night the Lord was betrayed, it would appear the Lord instituted what is now known as the "Lord's Supper" by taking up the third cup, traditionally known as the "cup of redemption" (Luke 22:20). Some take the Lord's words, "Do this in remembrance of me," to indicate His call for the continuance of the Seder meal in the Church (Luke 22:19). While that might be taking it too far, it is clear that the Seder serves as a foundation for understanding the Lord's Supper. This accounts for why many Christians who have attended Passover Seder presentations testify to having received a heightened understanding of the Lord's Supper after viewing it.

The Seder (as well as the other feasts) is a "shadow of the good things to come, the substance belongs to Christ" (Colossians 2:17). We will deal with this more thoroughly in Chapter 6. What is clear is that the Supper was meant to be an ongoing feast commemorating the true Lamb who was slain. It is also why the New Testament portrays the Lord's Supper as a full, covenantal meal, not merely the taking of the bread and the cup (although the bread and the cup are its main focus).

A Holy People

The Hebrew Bible teaches that Israel was a nation "set apart" to the Lord (Deuteronomy 7:6). After delivering them from Egyptian bondage by a mighty hand, He brought them to a mountain, where He entered into covenant with them. This setting apart of the nation to God embodies the idea behind the word "holy." To be holy is to be separated for a special purpose.

This idea of being separate is not what most people think of when they hear the word holy. To most, the word carries a moral significance; a purity of heart or being without sin. While the biblical idea behind the term certainly includes morality and purity, that's not its primary meaning. To be holy is to be separated from common use so as to be set apart for special use. For Israel as a nation, it meant being separated out from the nations and brought unto God (Exodus 19:4). This was the purpose for which God redeemed; that they may belong to Him. While the entire earth belonged to Him, they were His "treasured possession among all peoples" (Exodus 19:5).

We learn much about the meaning of holiness by observing God's dealings with Israel in the Old Testament. While God set Israel apart by His choice of them, it was as they responded to His calling that holiness was reflected in their lives. This separation (holiness) to the Lord was manifest in the most mundane issues of life, such as what they were to eat and drink and even the clothes they wore. And in all of these things, it was obvious that this was no ordinary nation but one set apart to God in every way. It was in this separation unto God that Israel understood its mission; *to mediate the glory of God to the nations.* Only by separating themselves *from* the nations could they fulfill their destiny to make known the true nature of the living God *to* the nations. As we know from the Old Testament, Israel failed miserably in this matter. Instead of reflecting the nature of the living God before the nations, they became like the other nations. But even this failure was not without purpose. It underscored the weakness of the Old Covenant in producing true holiness, thus demonstrating the need for a New Covenant whereby true separation might actually be realized.

The same call to holiness given to Israel in the Old Testament is now given to the Church in the New Covenant. But this is true holiness, whereas that offered to Israel under the Old Covenant was a mere shadow (1 Peter 1:15-16, Colossians 2:16). Only as God by the Spirit circumcises the heart and takes up residence within His people is true holiness achieved. But that doesn't mean that the earthly shadows are of no use; they do serve a significant purpose in foreshadowing the holiness that would one day be realized under the New Covenant. That is why almost all of the statements describing holiness found in the New Testament are borrowed from the Old. For example, in one verse in 1 Peter, the apostle pulls from many different Old Testament statements previously used of Israel alone to describe New Covenant believers,

> But you are a chosen race, a royal priesthood, a holy
> nation, a people for his own possession, that you
> may proclaim the excellencies of him who called
> you out of darkness into his marvelous light.
>
> — 1 Peter 2:9

These terms, used previously of Israel, are now descriptive of the Church of the redeemed. The shadow has now given rise to the Substance.

Looking Ahead

As you can see, the Church owes much to the Jewish people. Without them, we would not have a sacred canon, a true knowledge of God, a proper understanding of peoplehood, a commemorative Supper, or a real understanding of being separated unto the Lord. In each of these instances, God has used the Jewish people to prepare the Church for the reality which has come in the Messiah. And as much as the HRM emphasizes these things, it serves an important purpose for the Christian Church.

What then is the problem with the HRM if it serves to remind us of these things? The problem lies in their refusal to see these things as a mere *shadow* of the good things that have come in the Messiah. Instead of embracing the Substance, HRM teachers insist that believers continue to practice these things as evidence they belong to the people of God. This is especially the case when it comes to observing the Old Testament Feasts. Many HRM teachers insist that Gentile believers in the first century also kept the Feasts, and therefore they (non-Jewish believers) should today as well.

To make the case that Gentiles ought to keep the Feasts, many HRM teachers point to Emperor Constantine, who (according to them) intentionally extricated the faith from its Hebrew root system. Before Constantine, both Jewish and non-Jewish believers observed such things as the Saturday Sabbath and the Old Testament Feasts, but (in their view) Constantine radically changed all that. By the time he was done implementing his radical changes, the Christian faith was barely recognizable.

But is this an accurate portrayal of what actually happened? Did Constantine bring about the depths of change many HRM teachers portray? The next section attempts to answer this question and others as well by first examining what the first-century Jewish apostles required the churches they planted to practice. We begin by reviewing what actually occurred at the Jerusalem Conference and what it meant for Gentile believers (Acts 15). Too often, HRM teachers blame Constantine for these changes without carefully examining the outcome of the decisions made at the Jerusalem Conference for non-Jewish believers. While it is true that Constantine made radical changes to the Church during his lifetime, many of those changes were actually rooted in decisions that emerged out of the Conference. In the five chapters that follow, we will look at what the record reveals regarding these things.

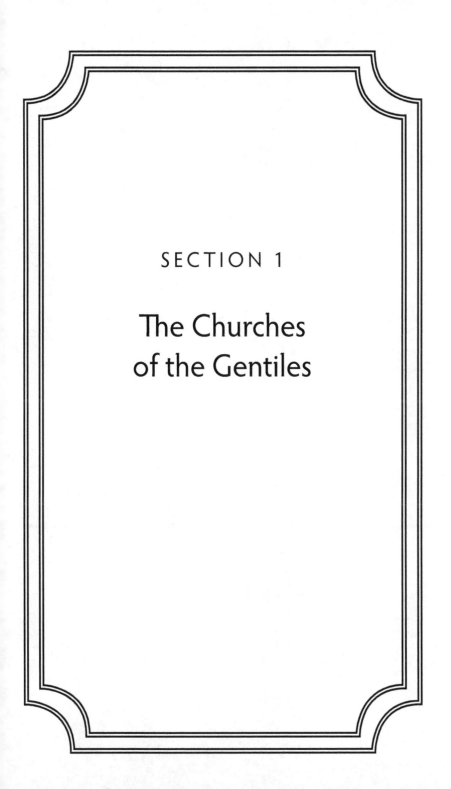

SECTION 1

The Churches
of the Gentiles

CHAPTER 3

The Jerusalem Conference: What It Meant for the Churches

The HRM is spreading rapidly throughout the world today, largely among non-Jewish believers who welcome its underlying message that the Church must be reconciled to its true root system. The HRM teaches that these roots extend back into Judaism rather than the paganism much of the modern church practices. While within the wider HRM, there are many varied practices, there is basic agreement on this; that believers must abandon modern Christianity and find in Hebraic forms and functions the true expression of the faith.

It is not surprising that Jewish believers in Jerusalem and Judea in the first century continued to practice their newfound faith in Jesus the Messiah within the context of Judaism. James (probably the earliest writing in the New Testament) addresses believers as still meeting in synagogues (the Greek word for assembly in James 2:2 is "sunagoge," meaning a formal gathering of Jews in a synagogue congregation). Many Gentile believers today assume that when Jews in the first century came to faith in Jesus as the Messiah, they abandoned their practice of such things as the Saturday Sabbath and started immediately meeting in churches for Sunday worship. But the record of the New Testament demonstrates otherwise.

When Paul came to Jerusalem, he was told by James and the other apostles that thousands of Jews believed and that they were all "zealous for the Law" (Acts 21:20). It was these Jerusalem apostles that counseled Paul to keep the vow along with four men to demonstrate to the inhabitants of Jerusalem that there was nothing to the rumor that Paul himself no longer kept the Law (21:22-24). This demonstrates that first-century Jews naturally practiced their faith within the confines of the Jewish religion, even after coming to believe.

But what about Gentiles? What did the Jewish apostles of the first century (especially the apostle Paul, who was the apostle to the Gentiles) instruct non-Jewish believers to perform after coming to faith in Messiah Jesus? That is the question we will seek to answer in this section of this book. It is an important one because many HRM teachers today are instructing Gentiles who believe in the Jewish Messiah to observe such things as the weekly Sabbath, the Feasts, as well as other aspects of the Jewish lifestyle. In a word, under the guise of returning to their true roots, many Gentiles are now seeking to practice the Law as a means of living out a fully Jewish lifestyle.

The Question of the Gentiles

In the first century, the church at Jerusalem faced a reversal of what we currently face today. In that day, the question was what to do with Gentiles who were coming to faith in the Messiah. Many Jews believed these Gentiles must first become converts to Judaism before they could be received into the believing community. Today, it's the exact opposite, with Jewish believers being the minority in the Church. The question the Church asks today is, "What do we do with Jews who believe?" In the first century, it was not a strange thing that Jews believed in their own Messiah. The real mystery was that Gentiles had now put their faith in a Jewish Messiah.

The Jerusalem apostles were slow at first to recognize that God was calling Gentiles to Messianic faith, even though Jesus Himself made it clear during His earthly ministry. For example, in the Parable of the Wedding Feast, Jesus announced how those originally invited to the wedding (Jews) refused to respond and were consequently rejected. The king then instructed his messengers, "Go therefore to the main roads and invite to the wedding feast as many as you find" (Matthew 22:9). The call had originally gone out to the Jewish people, but since they refused, he was now calling Gentiles to enter the messianic kingdom.

The book of Acts bears this out. As the Gospel moved westward, more and more Gentiles began to fill the ranks of the churches until they became the majority. This was certainly the case in Antioch, where Jews first preached the Gospel of a crucified, risen Messiah to Greeks, many of whom heard and believed (Acts 11:19-21). This was the beginning of the establishment of Antioch as the second great center for Christianity in the ancient world. Undoubtedly, there were other Jews than Paul and Barnabas in the church at Antioch, but the majority were Gentiles, having no former connection to Judaism.

It was without question that Gentiles were now invited into the messianic kingdom; the only question was what to do with them after they entered. Previous to the coming of the Messiah, Gentiles would have to be circumcised and keep the Law to be part of Israel. So it is not surprising that after hearing Gentiles had come to faith, Luke records how Pharisees from Jerusalem came down to Antioch, teaching these Gentile believers they must now be circumcised and keep the Law to be saved (Acts 15:1). Paul and Barnabas vigorously debated these teachers, defending the Gospel of grace entrusted to them. Their message was that "neither circumcision counts for anything, nor uncircumcision, but a new creation" (Galatians 6:15). To demand circumcision and Torah observance after believing was not merely misguided; it was a departure from the Gospel.

While Paul and Barnabas were defending the Gospel of grace at Antioch, a Roman centurion named Cornelius, a God-fearing Gentile, received a vision during the hour of prayer of an angel telling him his prayer was heard and to "send men to Joppa and bring one Simon who is called Peter" (Acts 10:5-6). Cornelius obeyed and sent the men to Joppa. The next day as the messengers neared the city, Peter went up on the rooftop to pray and fell into a trance. A vision was given to him of a sheet falling from heaven containing all kinds of unclean animals with a voice telling him to "Rise Peter; kill and eat" (Acts 10:13b). The vision repeated three times, and each time Peter refused. As he pondered the meaning of this vision, the men Cornelius had sent arrived, and the Spirit told Peter, "Behold, three men are looking for you. Rise and go down and accompany them without hesitation, for I have sent them" (Acts 10:19b-20).

Peter journeyed to Caesarea with the men Cornelius had sent and entering his house, found a large number of Cornelius' household gathered, awaiting his arrival. Cornelius rehearsed the reason he had sent for Peter. Now, Peter fully realized what his vision on the rooftop meant: "Truly I understand that God shows no partiality, but in every nation anyone who fears him and does what is right is acceptable to him" (Acts 10:34b-35). Peter preached the Gospel to all gathered there, beginning with John's baptism and the Gospel history of Jesus Christ. While he was preaching the word, Cornelius and his household believed, evidenced by the fact that God now gave them the same gift of the Spirit that Peter and his fellow apostles received on the Day of Pentecost. Turning to those who had come from the circumcision with him, Peter asked the obvious question, "Can anyone withhold water for baptizing these people, who have received the Holy Spirit just as we have?" (Acts 10:47).

Later, when Peter returned to Jerusalem, the apostles called him on the carpet for entering the house of a Gentile (Acts 11:1-3). But Peter explained to them all the events which led to his coming to Cornelius' house and his reception of the Gospel, and how God demonstrated their full acceptance by giving them the same gift of the Holy Spirit the apostles had received at Pentecost. The Jerusalem apostles realized that God was now opening the door of faith to Gentiles (Acts 11:18). The Messiah's kingdom now included Gentiles alongside their Jewish counterparts.

Still, many Jewish believers continued to insist that these Gentiles first had to become fully Jewish before they could be received into the messianic kingdom. After Paul and Barnabas had no small debate with these teachers at Antioch (Acts 15:1-2), it was determined they would go to Jerusalem and sit down with the apostles and elders to examine this matter. Thus was convened the first major Church council in history. There would be many more throughout the two-thousand-year history of the Church, but this first one was the most important.

The Jerusalem Conference: Victory for the Gospel of Grace

It goes without saying that one of the most important matters settled at the Jerusalem Conference was that Gentiles were not required to be circumcised after believing. It was a day of triumph for the Pauline Gospel of the grace of God. The Gentiles, along with their Jewish counterparts, received righteousness, not by keeping the Law but by believing the Gospel alone.

In the Galatian letter, the apostle Paul speaks of having been given a special revelation to go to Jerusalem and submit his

Gospel to the apostles (Galatians 2:1-4). When he arrived, he refused to yield one inch to those who were teaching that faith in the Gospel alone was not sufficient but must also be accompanied by Torah observance (Galatians 2:4). At the conference, they first heard from Peter, who told how God opened the door to the Gentiles through him (Acts 15:7-11), followed by Paul and Barnabas, who also reported how God also opened the door for them to the Gentiles (Acts 15:12). The Jerusalem apostles and elders listened in amazement as they heard about the signs and wonders which God performed among the Gentiles. It was becoming clear that Gentiles, along with their Jewish counterparts, were *fully* justified through faith alone.

After Peter and Paul and Barnabas, James, the brother of the Lord who listened quietly while the others made their case, weighed in. While he listened to the others tell how God had used them to preach the Gospel to the Gentiles, his mind thought on the great prophecy of Amos in which God promised to rebuild the Tabernacle of David:

> After this I will return, and I will rebuild the tent
> of David that has fallen; I will rebuild its ruins, and
> I will restore it, that the remnant of mankind may
> seek the Lord, and all the Gentiles who are called
> by my name, says the Lord, who makes these things
> known from of old.
>
> — Acts 15:16-17

As James meditated on this great prophecy, he realized that the fallen tent of David was not the restoration of a physical tent such as that which David built on Mount Zion, but the reality of the presence of God through a New Covenant in which both Jew and Gentile have freedom of access. In other words, it was a clear picture of all that God provided under the New Covenant. Just as David, who though not being a Levite or high priest could enter the direct presence of God as he sat before the ark, so one day Gentiles also would have access as well to God's presence without having to pass through veils or stations of worship. Though living under an Old Covenant, David was given a glimpse, for a short time, of New Covenant mercies.

In the end, the Jerusalem Conference meant vindication for the Gospel of grace. The apostles and elders required nothing of the Gentiles except to abstain from those things which would have been offensive to the Jews; "things polluted by idols, and from sexual immorality, and from things that have been strangled, and from blood" (Acts 15:20b). Some have pointed out that these four things pertained to idolatry and would have rendered them odious with Jews. Apart from these things, the Gentiles were justified and made righteous in the same way as their Jewish counterparts, by faith alone. Paul's doctrine of justification by faith alone stood the test of time, recognized as the only way God made both Jews and Gentiles righteous.

The apostles and elders of the Jerusalem church now wrote a letter to the believing Gentiles telling them that they were free from circumcision and Law-keeping as a means of justification. Could anything be clearer? Circumcision, the ancient rite which God gave to Abraham and upon which Jews were distinguished from the Gentiles, was no longer required as a covenantal rite. The people of God were no longer determined by a mark in their flesh but by a changed nature through regeneration.

How the HRM Views
the Jerusalem Conference

Most HRM teachers today believe that the Jerusalem Conference has little to do with them since they are not teaching Gentiles must be circumcised in order to be saved (most males are circumcised at birth today anyway). Yet the Jerusalem Conference was not only about circumcision but addressed the whole matter of *law-keeping* as well. This is important because, while most HRM teachers agree that circumcision is no longer necessary for salvation, they are quick to point out that the Jerusalem Conference said nothing about the Gentile's ongoing relationship to the Law. In other words, they limit the conclusions of the conference as pertaining to circumcision *only*, not whether Gentiles are under obligation to keep the Law. According to many HRM teachers, the conference didn't address the Gentiles' ongoing need to keep the Law simply because they (Gentiles) had already been taught to keep it.

But were the Jerusalem Conference conclusions limited to circumcision alone? Peter Ditzel, in an online article entitled the "Hebraic Roots Movement," states the following:

> Scholars commonly and wrongly assume that
> what they call The Jerusalem Council in Acts 15
> addressed circumcision only. But notice this from
> the letter composed after the meeting: "They wrote
> these things by their hand: 'The apostles, the elders,
> and the brothers, to the brothers who are of the
> Gentiles in Antioch, Syria, and Cilicia: greetings.
> Because we have heard that some who went out
> from us have troubled you with words, unsettling
> your souls, saying, "You must be circumcised and

keep the law," to whom we gave no commandment" (verses 23-24, emphasis mine). In other words, this meeting, besides the question of circumcision, also settled that the Gentiles did not have to keep the law. Earlier in the meeting, speaking of this attempt to make the Gentiles keep the law, Peter said, "Now therefore why do you tempt God, that you should put a yoke on the neck of the disciples which neither our fathers nor we were able to bear?" (verse 10, emphasis mine). Peter called the law a yoke on the neck, and he spoke of even the Jews' keeping of it in the past tense.[1]

The idea, therefore, that the conference only addressed the issue of circumcision is negated by the fact that the apostles were responding to those who were teaching that Gentiles "must be circumcised *and keep the Law*" (Acts 15:5). James, Peter, Paul, and the rest of the apostles responded in a straightforward manner, refuting that any such command or teaching came from them. Their letter (which they wrote to the Gentile churches) vindicated the Gospel by declaring that Gentiles were free from circumcision and Torah observance as a basis for being justified in Christ. There was nothing in the letter that suggested that while they were free from circumcision, they were still bound to keep the Law.

Yet, that is precisely what many HRM teachers are preaching and teaching today. For example, on Jim Staley's Passion for Truth website, he states the following:

What God destroyed on the cross was the penalty that the Law of God demanded as payment for the breaking of it... The Law of God was never abolished... And what was changed and "done away with" was the priestly system of sacrifices... We believe that believers today are to live their lives exactly the way the first-century believers lived: They kept the Torah as best as they could through the Spirit of Yeshua Messiah.[2]

See how Staley describes how the early believers at Jerusalem lived the Christian life—"keeping the Torah as best as they could through the Spirit of Yeshua Messiah?" He ignores Peter's reference to the Law as a "yoke on the disciple's neck," keeping them in bondage (Acts 15:10). Peter made no reference to the need for the Gentiles to remain under the yoke of the Law.

Shortly after the Jerusalem Conference, Paul describes how Peter enjoyed open fellowship with the Gentiles after coming to Antioch, something Orthodox Jews would never engage in previous to the coming of the Gospel. But when certain men arrived from Jerusalem, Peter immediately withdrew from fellowship with the Gentiles, giving the impression that the Law was still the dividing line between Jews and Gentiles. When Paul saw this, he openly rebuked Peter for his duplicity. Peter Ditzel points out that one version of the Bible translates verse 14 in such a way that Peter was compelling the nations to Judaize:

The Literal Translation of the Holy Bible ends verse 14 this way: "Why do you compel the nations to Judaize?" Peter had been living without the law, living as the Gentiles do. And, from what Paul says, it was obviously wrong for Peter to act in a way that put pressure on the Gentiles to live like the Jews. But what did we read above from the Hebraic Roots Movement? "The first-century believers...

kept the Torah as best as they could." Rubbish!
This is an attempt to put a yoke on your neck that
even the Jews were not able to bear. First-century
Christians—at least those who were not Judaizers—
knew that Christ fulfilled the law and that they
were saved by grace alone.[3]

It takes serious bias to reinterpret these words as supporting
the idea that believers tried their best to keep the Law. What the
conference established once for all is that non-Jewish believers
(as well as Jewish believers) were free from the Law to serve the
Messiah. The Jerusalem Conference did not just settle the matter
of circumcision but the relationship of the believer to the Law
as well. Believers were freed from the Law of Moses, now being
under the law of Messiah (1 Corinthians 9:21).

In the eighth chapter of the letter to the Romans, the apostle
Paul describes how believers now fulfill the Law:

> For God has done what the law, weakened by the
> flesh, could not do. By sending his own Son in the
> likeness of sinful flesh and for sin, he condemned
> sin in the flesh, in order that the righteous
> requirement of the law might be fulfilled in us, who
> walk not according to the flesh but according to the
> Spirit.
>
> — Romans 8:3-4

Paul says that the "righteous requirement of the law" is now
fulfilled in us who have the Spirit. That's because the Spirit always
leads us to observe the righteousness of the law in accordance
with the new nature of the believer who has the Spirit residing
within the believer. While the New Covenant believer is not

under the Law as a covenant, he is under the "law of Christ," which leads to fulfilling the righteousness of the Law.

Paul and Peter Face-Off at Antioch

In the letter Paul wrote to the Galatians, the truth that the Jerusalem apostles did not require law-keeping for Gentile believers is further confirmed. In fact, this entire letter was written against the charge that non-Jewish believers were required to keep the Law. Paul defends the Jerusalem Conference decision that Gentiles were not required to keep the Law and, in so doing, defends the truth of the grace of the Gospel. Men and women are not justified by anything they can do (Law-keeping) but by faith in the Messiah alone.

As was previously mentioned, after the Jerusalem Conference, Peter came to Antioch to visit Paul and the church there. During his visit, he moved freely among the Gentiles, eating the same foods and fellowshipping with them (Galatians 2:12). But when certain men showed up from Jerusalem, Peter was afraid and withdrew from table fellowship with the Gentiles. Due to his stature as leader of the apostolic twelve, other Jews such as Barnabas followed Peter's example and also withdrew from Gentile fellowship.

Paul, recognizing Peter's hypocrisy, confronted him publicly. But we should take careful notice of what Paul said to him. He identified that Peter lived like the Gentiles before certain men arrived from Jerusalem: "If you, though a Jew, live like a Gentile and not like a Jew, how can you force the Gentiles to live like Jews?" (Galatians 2:14b). In other words, Peter had previously been living as one who was not under the Law and therefore did not require Law-keeping of the Gentiles. But when he withdrew from the Gentiles, he was saying that he couldn't fellowship with those who did not first become Jews. Remember the way in which the literal translation of the Bible translates Galatians 2:14: "Why do you compel the nations to Judaize?" Paul says that it is hypocritical of Peter because he was requiring that the Gentiles Judaize.

But that is exactly what many HRM teachers are telling their non-Jewish followers they must now do—become Torah-observant, keep the Jewish Feasts and the Sabbath, as well as some other aspects of the Law. While they are quick to point out that believers do not have to do this in order to be justified, they are so concerned that Gentiles live like Jews; the message of salvation by grace alone through faith alone gets lost in the wash. What would Paul say today to HRM teachers who instruct Gentiles they must first become Jews if they want to be restored to the original root system of Christianity? Would he not condemn them as perverting the Gospel even as he withstood Peter to his face for his duplicity?

Believers Are Under the Law of Christ

If Gentiles, as well as Jewish believers, are not under the Law of Moses, what then are they under? Paul states clearly in another letter that he is under the law of Christ (1 Corinthians 9:21). In this passage, the apostle teaches that though a Jew, he acted as if he were still under the law at times. But right in the middle of that statement (in brackets), we find the words, "though I myself am not under law" (1 Corinthians 9:20, HCSB). Did you hear that? Paul no longer saw himself as under the law of Moses but under the law of Christ. Listen to what author Charles Leiter says about this:

> It is difficult for us to grasp just how radical these
> words were when they were first penned almost
> two thousand years ago. For every Jew of the first

century, the human race consisted of two (and only two) categories: Jew and Gentile. But in these verses, Paul—who had grown up in the strictest sect of Judaism, a "Pharisee of the Pharisees"— separates himself from both groups. He speaks of "the Jews" as "those who are under the Law" and of the Gentiles as "those who are without law," but he makes it very clear that he belongs to neither group. As a Christian, he is neither "under the Law" nor "without law"; instead, he is "under the law of Christ." That is, Paul no longer thinks of godly living in terms of the Mosaic Covenant, nor does he give himself to ungodly license; rather, his heart and mind are now focused on Christ.[4]

If that is true for Paul, the ex-Pharisee who was blameless as pertains to the Law (Philippians 3:6), how much more is it for Gentiles. The reason that Gentiles were not required to be circumcised in order to be saved is they were not required to be under the Law of Moses. Rather, they were under the law of Christ, which James calls the law of liberty (James 1:25). That doesn't mean that the law of Moses has no value for the true believer; it has much to teach us about God and His ways. But the believer is no longer under it *covenantally*, as a way of achieving righteousness. Many HRM teachers will agree with this in theory but still act and speak as though they are under the Law of Moses. While they parrot that the believer is not justified by Torah observance, they teach that the Law is essential for achieving sanctification. But Scripture (along with Christian experience) teaches that if we approach sanctification on the basis of the Law rather than by faith, we will struggle to live it out. It is only as the Holy Spirit works in our hearts through faith in the Gospel that we can truly live a sanctified life.

Do you see what Paul is saying? The righteous requirement of the Law is now fulfilled in believers who "do not walk according to the flesh but according to the Spirit" (Romans 8:4b). In other words, the righteousness the Law demands is now exhibited by a believer as he or she walks in the Spirit. Paul reminds the believers at Galatia that as they walk by the Spirit, they are no longer under the Law but under the law of Christ (Galatians 5:18).

Some have accused Paul of *antinomianism*, a term meaning "against law." Antinomianism is the belief that Christians are released by grace from the obligation of observing the moral law. Many of those who embrace this teaching use it to justify sinful lifestyles. But in the verse from Corinthians referred to previously, the apostle says, "To those outside the law I became as one outside the law (not being outside the law of God but under the law of Christ) that I might win those outside the law" (1 Corinthians 9:21). Notice how quickly Paul corrects himself when describing himself as being "outside the law." He doesn't mean he now lives his life outside of any law but under the "law of Christ." So far from being antinomian, Paul is teaching that he lives his life under the law of Christ.

What Lies Ahead

What exactly did that mean for Gentiles who had become believers in a Jewish Messiah? What was expected of them as far as observing such things as the Old Testament Feasts and the Sabbath Day? We will look at that more closely in two chapters of this section. But first, we must carefully examine a major HRM belief; that Gentiles in the early church, for at least the first three centuries, celebrated the Old Testament Feast days and the weekly Sabbath until a Roman emperor came to the throne in the early fourth century and changed things forever.

It is true that Constantine made fundamental changes to the medieval Church when he began to involve himself in its affairs. But as I hope to make clear, some of the claims HRM teachers make regarding the extrication of the faith from its Hebrew root system by Constantine are greatly exaggerated. More about that in the next chapter.

CHAPTER 4

Did Constantine Change Everything?

The story of Constantine and his influence on the Christian Church has been written about (and argued over) for seventeen centuries. The arguments have largely revolved around whether or not Constantine's conversion to Christianity was genuine. Some hold that God gave him a supernatural sign which led to genuine faith in Jesus. Others see his embrace of Christianity as largely a political ploy aimed at gaining control of the Christian church. Those on each side of the debate have their so-called evidence for their position.

What Constantine himself reports is that as he was going out to the Battle of Milvian Bridge in AD 312, he looked up at the sun and saw a cross of light above it, and with it the Greek words, "In this sign, conquer!" Constantine commanded his troops to adorn their shields with this Christian symbol and thereafter was victorious. Following the battle, the new emperor ignored the altars to the gods and did not carry out the customary sacrifices to celebrate a general's victorious entry into Rome. Instead, he headed directly to the imperial palace and embraced the religion which had previously been outlawed. He turned over confiscated property back to its Christian owners and relaxed the ban on Christianity. From that moment, Constantine showed great tolerance towards the faith which had previously been persecuted, taking an active part in influencing the direction of the Church in the Empire.

In AD 325, Constantine convened a council of Christian bishops at Nicea to settle some important theological issues threatening to tear apart the delicate unity of the faith. For the first time in history, a Roman emperor took a leading role in preserving Christian unity! This is amazing, especially in light of the fact that Diocletian, who reigned prior to Constantine in AD 244-312, bitterly opposed the Church, persecuting it fiercely. Some of the bishops who attended the Nicean Council bore in their bodies the marks of Diocletian's persecutions. How mesmerized they must have been to now be sitting in a hall with a Roman emperor not only sympathetic to the faith but directly involved in its affairs.

Nicea settled some of the most important issues facing the Church, such as the deity of Christ and the triune nature of God (the Trinity). What emerged was a unified Church that condemned heresy and established the first acceptable creed known as the Nicene Creed. While only approximately 18 percent of the bishops attended, the decisions of that council were far-reaching and are still impacting us today. To this day, the Nicene Creed is considered one of the most important Christian documents ever written.

Many Church History teachers have suggested that unless Constantine had come along, Christianity would have been defeated in the Empire. But Robert Arakaki, in an article entitled "Constantine the Great: Roman Emperor, Christian Saint, History's Turning Point," puts this into proper perspective:

> Contrary to popular belief, Constantine did not
> rescue Christianity from extinction. Even if he had

not adopted the Christian cause, the majority of the Roman population was well on its way to becoming Christian. What Constantine did do was hasten the process of evangelizing the Roman Empire. Constantine's conversion marked the climax of a centuries-long process of evangelization that began in an obscure corner of the Roman Empire. For the first time, the entire structure of Roman civilization, from the emperor down to the lowest slave, shared the Christian faith.[1]

It's not surprising that most HRM teachers view Constantine negatively, blaming him for intentionally severing the faith from its Jewish roots by changing the Sabbath to Sunday and establishing the Christian doctrine of the Trinity. In a word, many HRM teachers blame Constantine for making Christianity pagan. According to these teachers, the Church was well connected to its Hebrew root system until Constantine severed it from that root, replacing it with pagan ideas and observances. For example, he took a pagan festival celebrated on December 25th, which commemorated the birth of Mithras, the Persian god of light, and merged it with the Nativity story in the Bible (sorry to ruin your Christmas).

It goes without saying that Constantine did mix pagan ideas with Christianity. But as I hope to make evident in this chapter, many in the HRM have gone too far in blaming him for mixing pagan ideas and practices into the faith.

Nicene and the Trinity

One example of the HRM going too far is the belief that the doctrine of the Trinity, formulated at the Council of Nicaea, was invented by Constantine rather than being a summary of the teaching of the apostles. While it is true that the term (Trinity) itself is not found in Scripture, the concept is biblical. Let me explain.

The central reason Constantine initiated the Council of Nicea was to settle the theological issue spawned by the teaching of a bishop named Arius. Among other things, Arius taught that Jesus Christ was a created being, not the very God of gods. This was no minor issue as Church Father Athanasius stated clearly, "If Christ were not truly God, then he could not bestow life upon the repentant and free them from sin and death" (Saint Athanasius). So this was more than just a minor squabble over terms—the Gospel itself was at stake. If Christ was not God of gods, then His blood was unable to save anyone. This should place Nicea as one of the most important events in Christendom, second perhaps to the Jerusalem Council itself.

Those opposed to the doctrine of the Trinity claim that Constantine forced this doctrine on the Church. It is true that Constantine oversaw this Council and that the doctrine of the Trinity was upheld. Nevertheless, Constantine did not invent Trinitarianism; he merely codified the beliefs of the Church regarding it through the first few centuries. In his paper entitled *"Did Constantine Invent the Trinity?: The Doctrine of the Trinity in the Writings of the Early Church Fathers*, Nathan Busenitz, an Instructor of Theology, said the following:

> Opponents of the doctrine of the Trinity often
> claim that it was an invention of Emperor
> Constantine at the Council of Nicaea. This goes
> against much evidence that the early church fathers
> affirmed the Trinity. The ante-Nicene church fathers

acknowledged that there is only one God. Yet
they also taught that the Godhead consists of the
Father, the Son, and the Holy Spirit—three distinct
Persons, each of whom is God.[2]

Another issue many HRM adherents have with the Nicene
Council is their belief that it is blatantly "anti-Jewish." David
Stern references this blatant anti-Jewish tendency when he
refers to the reasons many Jewish believers left their people after
coming to faith in Jesus:

> Why, in the past, did many Jewish believers, in
> practice, leave their people? Because in the fourth
> century, when Roman Emperor Constantine
> converted to Christianity, and the Gentile-
> dominated Church gained political power, it began
> to require Jews who accepted Yeshua as the Messiah
> to give up all ties with Judaism, Jewish practices,
> Jewish friends and anything Jewish.[3]

There is almost no denying that what Stern is saying here
is accurate. But it is easy to focus on these atrocities to such a
degree; we cease to see the great benefit to Christianity achieved
by Constantine. Defending the deity of the Jewish Messiah
from outside attacks while formulating an understanding of the
Godhead that would serve the Church of God for centuries to
come is no small feat. We can appreciate these things without
minimizing the atrocious behavior the Church has exhibited
towards the Jewish people and their contribution.

The Trinity: Manmade Concoction or Revelation?

We still must answer the question, "Did Nicea invent the trinitarian concept of the Godhead?" Accepting the fact that Nicea was a mixed bag when it came to human traditions mixed with political aspiration and theological positions, what exactly did Nicea accomplish? Don Closson, in an online article entitled "Did the Emperor Constantine Impose the Doctrine of the Trinity on the Council of Nicea?" puts it in perspective:

> A common criticism by those who reject the doctrine of the Trinity is that the doctrine was not part of the early church, nor conscious teaching of Jesus Himself, but was imposed on the church by Emperor Constantine in the early fourth century at the Council of Nicea. Mormons argue that components of Constantine's pagan thought and Greek philosophy were forced on the bishops who assembled in Nicea (located in present-day Turkey). Jehovah's Witnesses believe that the Emperor weighed in against their view, which was the position argued by Arius at the council, and, again, forced the church to follow.[4]

One of the clearest ways we know that the doctrine of the Trinity was not invented at Nicea is the simple fact that Jesus Himself referenced the triune God during his earthly ministry. Take, for example, his reference to Father, Son, and the Holy Spirit when issuing the Great Commission, which served as a baptismal formula for Christian baptism. Yet besides Jesus' teaching, also consider how the Didache, an early second-century

Christian instruction manual, contains a trinitarian baptismal formula as well. New believers were asked to be baptized in the name of the Father, His Son, Jesus Christ, and the Holy Spirit, thus affirming their faith in the trinitarian idea of the Godhead.

But there is also another factor that helps to solidify the fact that the Church was Trinitarian before Constantine, as Don Closson further explains:

> Finally, the bishops who attended the Council of Nicea were far too independent and toughened by persecution and martyrdom to give in so easily to a doctrine they didn't agree with. As we have already mentioned, many of these bishops were banished by emperors supporting the Arian view and yet held on to their convictions. Also, the Council at Constantinople in 381 reaffirmed the Trinitarian position after Constantine died. If the church had temporarily succumbed to Constantine's influence, it could have rejected the doctrine at this later council.[5]

So taken together, there is no evidence that the Church rejected the Trinitarian view of the Godhead until it was forced to accept it by Constantine at the Council of Nicea. If anything, it would appear that Nicea, far from forcing Trinitarianism upon the Church, simply summarized the teaching of the Church for the first three hundred years.

Looking Ahead

What about Constantine's decree that Sunday be observed as the Roman day of rest? It was no doubt modeled on pagan sun worship (though he wanted it to benefit the Church). Was Constantine not changing the Jewish Sabbath from Saturday to Sunday? If so, that means the churches of the Gentiles continued to gather on the Saturday Sabbath until Constantine forced them to change. We will take that up in our next chapter.

CHAPTER 5

Entering His Rest

In the first chapter of this book, I recounted my conversation with Ralph, a member of our church who embraced teaching, promising to reconnect him to the true roots of the faith. Although Ralph still came to our church on Sundays, I warned him that if he weren't careful, he would eventually abandon worship on the Lord's Day for Saturday worship. Ralph strongly disagreed, yet despite my warning, he and his family eventually drew back from Sunday worship, choosing instead to meet with a group that worshipped exclusively on Saturday.

Many HRM teachers believe and teach that authentic Christian worship requires believers to observe the weekly Saturday Sabbath. On a trip to Israel a few years ago, I met a Gentile believer in Jerusalem who spoke to our group about the blessing he has received since becoming a Sabbath observer. And he is not alone. Many non-Jewish believers have testified to the blessings they have enjoyed by worshipping on the right day. That is why so many Gentile believers in Jesus believe it is God's will for them to observe the Saturday Sabbath.

But isn't the Sabbath part of the Law which has been done away with in Christ? Many point to the fact that the Sabbath was not instituted at Sinai but at Creation to defend the practice of believers keeping it today. They remind us that when God introduced the command to observe the Sabbath on Sinai, it was preceded by the word "remember" (Exodus 20:8). Israel was to remember what God had already given (see Genesis 2:1-4). So the Sabbath ordinance predates the Law, having been instituted as part of the original creation.

We should not find it surprising, therefore, that the early Jewish believers in Jerusalem continued to observe the Saturday Sabbath after becoming believers in Jesus as the Messiah. As Jews, Sabbath observance was a major part of their religious life. Many Christians today have the idea that when Jews first believed in Jesus as the Messiah, they immediately dropped their Jewish customs for Christian ones, such as Christian worship on Sundays in church buildings and Lord's Supper observance. Yet as the book of Acts points out, Jews who believed in Jesus as the Messiah continued to worship on the Sabbath, keep the feasts, and gather in the temple. (Acts 2:46, Acts 21:20). In fact, Christianity had the protection of the Roman Empire for many years since it was at first viewed as a sect of Judaism. That is why congregations of Jewish believers in Israel today continue to meet and worship on the Sabbath rather than Sunday.

But what about the Gentile churches Peter, Paul, and John founded throughout the Roman Empire? Did they instruct the Gentile believers in those churches to keep the Jewish Sabbath as their Jewish counterparts did? According to many HRM teachers, the early apostles *did* instruct Gentile believers to keep the Sabbath until it was changed from Saturday to Sunday at the Council of Nicea. And they believe that if Gentile believers are to live out a pure faith today, they must continue to do so. In other words, non-Jewish believers should be worshipping on Saturdays rather than Sundays.

First, let's acknowledge that believers are free in the Messiah to observe one day above another, including the Saturday Sabbath (see Romans 14:5). But Paul is also adamant that believers must not allow personal convictions about such things as Sabbath-keeping and the observing of the feasts to become law others must follow. Yet, that is exactly what many HRM teachers today are doing. Since the Sabbath is a part of the Law and (according to them) believers are still under it, many HRM teachers insist that Sabbath observance is therefore binding for all, including Gentiles.

Sunday Is the Lord's Day, Not the Sabbath

Nowhere in Scripture is it taught either directly or indirectly that God changed the Sabbath day from Saturday to Sunday. The Sabbath continues to be the seventh day of the week, which is Saturday. Whatever Christians did on Sunday was never intended to be a replacement for the Sabbath.

Why then didn't the Gentile churches meet on the weekly Sabbath for worship like their Jewish counterparts? We will answer that more fully later in this chapter, but first, let's tackle the reason Christians in the first century met on Sunday (and continue to do so today). Then we will be in a better position to understand that God never intended Sunday to be a replacement for the weekly Saturday Sabbath.

It seems clear from the record that Gentile believers in the first century gathered on Sunday as their main day of worship, referring to it as the "Lord's Day" (Acts 20:7, 1 Corinthians 16:2, Revelation 1:10). Where did the tradition of Sunday being the Lord's Day originate? It would appear it was one of those things Christians borrowed from Rome and gave Christian meaning. There are numerous examples of such Christianization of Roman customs in the New Testament. The opening salutation, "grace and peace to you," found in many of the Pauline letters, appears to be a Christianized version of the Roman toast in the taverns. The Christian "love feast" was a sanctified version of the pagan feasts in celebration of the various gods Romans worshipped by sex orgies. The Christians said they also gathered to share love amongst themselves, not by practicing sexual immorality, but through a mutual sharing of the love of God at the love feasts.

What Roman custom did Christians use when referring to Sunday as the Lord's Day? It is possible it was the custom known as "Emperor" Day. Whatever day a Roman emperor came to his throne was known throughout his reign as "Emperor Day." Since Jesus came to His throne on Sunday (the day of his resurrection), that day became known as the "Lord's Day." It is no surprise, therefore, that they would gather on that day, not as a replacement of the Sabbath, but as the day to remember their King who came to His throne.

This, coupled with the fact that there are no commands by the apostles to Gentile believers to observe the Jewish Sabbath, makes it clear that Gentiles worshipped on the Lord's Day (Sunday). While the early chapters of Acts clearly demonstrate that Jewish believers kept the Saturday Sabbath, that is not what we see the Gentile churches practicing. For example, when the apostle Paul came to Troas, he stayed long enough to break bread with the church there. What day of the week was that? Luke tells us that the church was gathered together on the first day of the week (Sunday), "On the first day of the week, when we were gathered together to break bread, Paul talked with them, intending to depart on the next day, and he prolonged his speech until midnight" (Acts 20:7).

It seems unlikely that the church at Troas met only this one time on the first day of the week but rather referred to their regular practice. This corresponds with a passage in 1 Corinthians where the apostle mentions the special offering to be collected when the church was gathered "on the first day of the week" (1 Corinthians 16:2). The mention of this both at Troas and at Corinth seems to underscore that the churches regularly gathered on the first day of the week to worship and hear Christian teaching. Incidentally, Luke tells us that the church at Troas met on the first day of the week to "break bread," a reference to the traditional celebration of the Lord's Supper meal. This is incredible in the light of the fact that the apostle Paul was visiting while they were gathered. Luke doesn't say that the church at Troas gathered to hear Paul but to break bread. The fact that Paul was there was an added blessing.

We also have the testimony of the apostle John on the island of Patmos. He speaks of being "in the Spirit on the Lord's Day" when he was taken out of this earthly realm and given a vision of God unparalleled in Scripture. Scholars have debated for centuries what John meant by the phrase "the Lord's Day." Some believe it was a reference to the final Day of Judgment when the Lord Jesus comes and the wrath of God is completed. Yet, it is much more likely that John meant the traditional day in which Christians gathered to worship their King. Tradition says that John was allowed to remain in his cave and worship on Sunday while being imprisoned on the island of Patmos. Since he was unable to gather with his beloved churches in Asia due to his banishment, he was gathered with them in the Spirit. This may have been his regular practice.

Besides these Scriptural references, we also have the testimony of early Church Fathers of the first three centuries that the churches of the Gentiles regularly gathered on the first day of the week. Tertullian, the early Church Father writing around AD 200, said, "But why is it, you ask, that we gather on the Lord's Day to celebrate our solemnities? Because that was the way the Apostles also did."[1]

Ignatius, writing a full century earlier, said the following,

> Those who were brought up in the ancient order of
> things have come to the possession of a new hope,
> no longer observing the Sabbath, but living in the
> observance of the Lord's day on which our life was
> sprung by him and his death.[2]

If there is any doubt what these Church Fathers meant by the Lord's Day, Justin Martyr, writing in AD 140, clarifies,

> Sunday is the day on which we all hold our common
> assembly, because it is the day on which God, when
> he changed the darkness and matter, made the
> world; and Jesus Christ our Savior on the same day
> rose from the dead.[3]

And just in case there is any doubt as to what Justin Martyr meant, he made it even clearer, "We neither accord with the Jews in their peculiarities in regard to food nor in their sacred days."[4]

Justin Martyr was writing in AD 140, about forty or fifty years after John had died. He knew those who walked with the apostles themselves. So when he says that the churches gathered on Sunday to hear the records of the apostles and the writings of the prophets, he had access to those who were personally discipled by some of the apostles.

To be clear, the Fathers are not teaching that the Sabbath has been changed from Saturday to Sunday. The official Sabbath is still Saturday; the apostles never viewed Sunday as a replacement for the Sabbath (while undoubtedly some of the Church Fathers did). While it is clear that the first Jewish believers in Jerusalem kept the Saturday Sabbath, there is no evidence that the Jewish apostles instructed the Gentile churches to observe it. As we can see from the record of the Fathers, the Gentile churches met on Sunday to celebrate the resurrection.

The Sabbath and Constantine

Since we can see from the teaching of the apostles as well as the practice of the Gentile churches in the New Testament, the Gentile churches gathered on the Lord's Day. What exactly then did Emperor Constantine change when he ascended to the throne? Looking carefully, we find that while recognizing Sunday as the Lord's Day, he formally changed the observance of the Passover on the closest Sunday to the fourteenth rather than observing it on the fourteenth. The early churches observed Passover each year, which they called "Pascha" in Greek, a word meaning suffering and referring to Christ's suffering before and upon the cross. It was settled by the West practicing one thing while the East another.

What is important to note, though, is that while Constantine at Nicea did make a statement about worship on Sunday, it's simply not true that he changed the Saturday Sabbath to Sunday and ordered the churches to observe it. In the year AD 321, Constantine decreed, "On the venerable day of the Sun let the magistrates and people residing in cities rest, and let all workshops be closed."[5] Here is the fuller statement of what Constantine ordered:

> On the venerable Day of the Sun let the magistrates
> and people residing in cities rest, and let all
> workshops be closed. In the country, however,
> persons engaged in agriculture may freely and
> lawfully continue their pursuits; because it often
> happens that another day is not so suitable for grain

sowing or for vine-planting; lest by neglecting the proper moment for such operations the bounty of heaven should be lost.[6]

Sunday was called in paganism the "Day of the Sun." It is likely what Constantine did was to make it an official Christian holiday. But that is a far cry from saying that Constantine changed the Sabbath from Saturday to Sunday. Here are some details regarding the edict:

> The decree was far-reaching, stating that numerous activities should be avoided on Sunday. Merchants were forbidden to trade, and administrative establishments were closed, apart from those that dealt with the freeing of slaves. Farmers alone were permitted to continue working on the Sabbath, in recognition that some farm activity was impossible to defer. Constantine chose Sunday to be the day for Christian worship as it already enjoyed special status in the Roman week. Named after the Pagan Sun God Invictus, Sunday had become the day when wages were traditionally paid to workers, leading it to be seen as a day of celebration and thanks. In corresponding to the Christian Sabbath with an already established day of rest, Constantine ensured that his decree would be accepted swiftly and harmoniously.[7]

What About Colossians 2:16?

But this flies in the face of what many in the HRM believe; that Constantine changed the Saturday Sabbath to Sunday, thus causing the Gentiles churches to abandon their practice of worshipping on the Sabbath. Yet more important than trying to figure out what happened in the fourth century, it is first necessary to examine the clear statements of Scripture regarding Sabbath-keeping. In this regard, no other passage is as important as Colossians 2:16, which seems to clearly teach that believers are no longer obligated to keep the Saturday Sabbath: "Therefore let no one pass judgment on you in questions of food and drink, or with regard to a festival or a new moon or a Sabbath" (Colossians 2:16).

How do HRM teachers escape the fact that this reference to a Sabbath in this passage seems to clearly refer to the Saturday Sabbath? They do so by insisting that the Sabbath in this passage here is not to the regular weekly Sabbath but to the various sabbaths attached to the feasts. The fact that he lumps it together with other things (festival, new moon, Sabbath) could mean that Paul is referring to the other monthly Sabbaths, which were seen as temporary, and not the weekly Sabbath, which was permanent. As one author said:

> There were monthly sabbaths in the Israelite calendar. Those were purely temporary and typological. They were not part of the creational pattern but were purely Israelite. Unlike the creational pattern of setting aside one day in 7 for rest and worship, which was transformed by the inauguration of the new creation by Christ's resurrection, the monthly Israelite sabbaths were never intended to be perpetual.[8]

While it is true that there were other Sabbaths attached to the feasts and that Paul might be referring to them in this passage, that does not rule out that he is also referring to the regular, weekly Saturday Sabbath. For one thing, the word translated Sabbath in the text is *sabbaton*, the regular word used of the weekly Sabbath. In fact, the Greek word sabbaton is never used in the New Testament even once to refer to the ceremonial Sabbath days. The word is used sixty-two times in the New Testament, and every one of them refers to the weekly Sabbath.

But also, when comparing what Paul says in Colossians 2:16 with what the writer of Hebrews says in Hebrews chapter four, we find that there are similar threads. Writing to the Colossians, Paul tells them that everything in the Old Covenant—festival, new moon, and Sabbath was a shadow of things to come, but the substance belongs to Christ (Colossians 2:17). And that is the message of the book of Hebrews. The Law, according to the writer, is but a *shadow* of the good things to come" (Hebrews 10:1; italics mine). That means that the Sabbath was a shadow of a spiritual reality that came at the appearing of the Messiah.

In chapter four of Hebrews, the writer picks up on this, applying it specifically to the Sabbath. He quotes directly from Genesis 2: "So God blessed the seventh day and made it holy, because on it God rested from all his work that he had done in creation" (Genesis 2:3). The chapter is not about literal Sabbath-keeping but God's invitation that His people enter His eternal rest. The phrase "So then, there remains a Sabbath rest for the people of God" (Hebrews 4:9) is not a call to keep the literal Sabbath, but to enter into the finished work of the Messiah, "for whoever has entered God's rest has also rested from his works as God did from his" (Hebrews 4:10). Here, the Messiah is presented as finishing the work of redemption in the same way God finished his work of creation, after which he invited his creatures to enter his rest (Genesis 2:1-4). In the same way, after the Messiah accomplished eternal redemption, He sat down at the right hand of the Majesty on high from which He now invites His own to enter His completed work and rest forever.

The Sabbath Was a Sign

One important aspect of the Saturday Sabbath when it was given to Israel is that it served as a sign in the same way circumcision served as a sign:

> And God said to Abraham, "As for you, you shall keep my covenant, you and your offspring after you throughout their generations. This is my covenant, which you shall keep, between me and you and your offspring after you: Every male among you shall be circumcised. You shall be circumcised in the flesh of your foreskins, and it shall be a sign of the covenant between me and you."
>
> — Genesis 17:9-11 (italics added)

Notice how God refers to circumcision as a "*sign* of the covenant." Also, notice the fact that he uses the exact same language to describe the Sabbath:

> And the LORD said to Moses, "You are to speak to the people of Israel and say, 'Above all you shall keep my Sabbaths, for this is a sign between me and you throughout your generations, that you may know that I, the LORD, sanctify you. Therefore, the people of Israel shall keep the Sabbath, observing

the Sabbath throughout their generations, as a covenant forever. It is a sign forever between me and the people of Israel that in six days the LORD made heaven and earth, and on the seventh day he rested and was refreshed'"

— Exodus 31:12-13, 16-17

Charles Leiter explains what is meant by this idea that the Sabbath was a sign:

> The fact that the Sabbath was given to Israel as a sign of the Mosaic Covenant explains its place of prominence among 'the words of the covenant, the Ten Commandments.' There is a sense in which the Sabbath's place in the Mosaic Covenant is similar to a wedding ring's place in the marriage covenant. Just as a wife's taking off her wedding ring and throwing it at her husband has a far deeper significance than the outward action itself might seem to imply, even so, any Jew's deliberate breaking of the Sabbath Day was considered by God to be a very grave offense, punishable by death.[9]

The Sabbath was a sign of the covenant and, therefore, was extremely important. But like circumcision, it has now been swallowed up in the reality which has come in Christ. It is part of the shadow that was given to reflect the substance, the reality that just as God rested after all His work, so Christ now rests, inviting us to enter it.

Should We Observe the Day?

As a pastor over the years, I have made it a regular practice to preach through the fourteenth chapter of Romans at least once a year. In my mind, it is one of the greatest expositions on the practical effects grace should have on our lives. We learn from this chapter that the grace of God produces different convictions regarding our private practices concerning such things as drinking wine and eating meat offered to idols. Believers are free in the Messiah to practice (or not practice) these various things. The important thing is that each is living in accordance with the personal convictions grace has produced in their consciences, without demanding others live by the same convictions. This includes differing convictions on which days one should observe.

While the word Sabbath is not mentioned directly, it seems to be alluded to in verse five: "One person esteems one day as better than another, while another esteems all days alike" (Romans 14:5a). Keep in mind that the church in Rome was comprised of both Jewish and Gentile believers. It isn't difficult, therefore, to see that Paul here refers to Jews who held the seventh day sacred ("one person esteems one day as better than another") and Gentiles who esteemed them all the same ("while another esteems all days alike"). What is clear in this passage is that due to the grace of God working in their consciences, some felt the need to observe certain days in a special way, while others treated every day alike. Each was to be fully persuaded in his or her mind as to what God would have them do.

That means that believers are free in Christ to keep the weekly Saturday Sabbath if their conscience dictates as long as they do so in keeping with the principles Paul enumerates. First, they must be fully persuaded that this is something God wants them to do, not as a matter of obtaining salvation but as a result of receiving the grace of God. Second, each believer must realize that these convictions are personal and cannot be forced on others. In other words, they must hold these things as private preferences, never allowing themselves to judge others who have different convictions.

But that is what rarely happens among believers (hence the necessity of Paul's teaching here in Romans 14). I knew of a church where the pastor developed a personal conviction not to own a television set. While he never preached that everyone in the congregation should toss their sets, there was a subtle innuendo that if you are really spiritual, you wouldn't own one. Thus, a personal conviction of one person became the standard by which all others were judged (a clear violation of what Paul teaches in Romans 14). It may have been wisdom to appeal to others about the benefit of not owning a set, but when one's spirituality is judged in the light of whether or not they own a television, it has subtly (or not so subtly) moved from the realm of personal conviction to a commandment all are obligated to obey.

How much more difficult it must have been in the Church at Rome where Jews were fastidious about keeping the seventh day, while Gentiles viewed each day the same. Nevertheless, Paul insists that each believer must hold his own convictions personally while respectfully giving grace to those who hold differing convictions. Did Paul mean that Jewish believers were free to observe the Sabbath as long as they refused to force the Gentiles to observe it as well? It seems that that is the case. Earlier in this chapter, I gave reasons why I believe Scriptures such as Romans 14:5, Colossians 2:16, and Hebrews 4 are referring to the Saturday Sabbath as well as other feast days. In a congregation such as Rome with both Jews and Gentiles, it is reasonable to assume that Paul is referring to Jews who observed one day above another and Gentiles who esteemed each day alike.

Yet, that is not how most HRM teachers today approach the Sabbath. They deny that Colossians 2:16 refers to the weekly Saturday Sabbath, but only to the sabbath days that were part of the various feasts celebrated throughout Israel's calendar year. They believe, therefore, that not only Jewish believers should be keeping the weekly Sabbath but Gentiles as well:

> The influence of this movement is dangerous in that they call Gentiles to a Torah-observant and/or festival observant lifestyle as a means of drawing closer to Yeshua and being conformed to His image. The implication is, "If you really want to please Yahweh, if you really want to be holy, here are the rules." Even though most do not believe these observances are necessary for one's salvation, there is often an implication that this is the higher way. Nowhere in the Bible do we find Gentile believers being instructed to follow Levitical laws or Jewish customs.[10]

Did you hear Pastor Curtis: "Nowhere in the Bible do we find Gentile believers being instructed to follow Levitical laws or Jewish customs" (Pastor Curtis). That is not entirely true, for the Judaizers at Galatia taught Gentile believers there they must be circumcised and keep the entire Law in order to be saved. The letter to the Galatians is Paul's defense against those who taught these things. No doubt, these teachers made the same arguments HRM teachers do today; that by being Torah-observant and festival observant (see next chapter), they would have a closer walk with Yeshua. But Paul demonstrates in Galatians that this teaching, far from being a boon to spiritual development, is a departure from the Gospel.

In this chapter, I have focused on the HRM emphasis on Sabbath-keeping. Most HRM teachers also teach that Gentile believers should be observing the Jewish feast days in place of the Christian holidays (Christmas and Easter), which they consider to be pagan. That is the focus of our next chapter.

CHAPTER 6

Let Us Keep the Feast

When God revealed Himself to Israel at Mount Sinai after delivering them from four hundred years of Egyptian bondage, one of the first things He did was to rearrange their calendar year. Certain days were designated as feast days to the Lord, set apart for worship (Exodus 23). The three central feasts—Passover, Pentecost (Feast of Harvest), and Tabernacles (Feast of Ingathering) required every male Israelite to journey to the place where the Lord God eventually would put His Name after inheriting the land:

> Three times in the year, you shall keep a feast to me. You shall keep the Feast of Unleavened Bread. As I commanded you, you shall eat unleavened bread for seven days at the appointed time in the month of Abib, for in it you came out of Egypt. None shall appear before me empty-handed. You shall keep the Feast of Harvest, of the first fruits of your labor, of what you sow in the field. You shall keep the Feast of Ingathering at the end of the year when you gather in from the field the fruit of your labor. Three times in the year shall all your males appear before the Lord God.
>
> — Exodus 23:14-17

There were other feasts as well, but these, along with the weekly Sabbath, marked Israel out as a special nation. There was no other nation on earth that observed their God with such visible displays of celebration. The beauty of celebrating these feasts was one of the main reasons many from the nations were drawn to the worship of Jehovah. Israel was commanded to celebrate these feasts annually as an expression of their being in covenant with God.

But this was under the Old Covenant. What is the relationship of these feasts to the people of God under the New Covenant? Is the Church of God now required to keep these feasts? Most HRM teachers today would answer affirmatively, pointing to the fact that when God instituted these feasts, he often referred to them as *permanent* observances (Passover was to be celebrated as a "statute forever.") (Exodus 12:17). For them, such language meant God never intended these feasts to cease being observed. Today, many HRM teachers believe that not only Jewish but Gentile believers should be observing them as well.

It is not surprising that many Jewish believers today continue to celebrate the feasts, having grown up with them. I look forward each year to our family Passover Seder as well as our annual lighting of our menorah at Hanukah. I don't observe them because I consider myself still under the Law but because I consider them to be one of the best ways of understanding the Gospel. They are part of the shadow language of the Old Testament and, as such, shed much light on the glory of the Substance which has come in Christ (Colossians 2:16, Hebrews 10:1).

But that is not the reason many HRM teachers today teach Gentiles to keep the feasts. Rather, many teach they should be observed as a covenantal obligation. For example, Scriptures such as Zechariah 14:16-19 are often used as a biblical basis for keeping the Feast of Tabernacles:

Then everyone who survives of all the nations that have come against Jerusalem shall go up year after year to worship the King, the LORD of hosts, and to keep the Feast of Booths. And if any of the families of the earth do not go up to Jerusalem to worship the King, the LORD of hosts, there will be no rain on them. And if the family of Egypt does not go up and present themselves, then on them there shall be no rain; there shall be the plague with which the Lord afflicts the nations that do not go up to keep the Feast of Booths. This shall be the punishment to Egypt and the punishment to all the nations that do not go up to keep the Feast of Booths.

— Zechariah 14:16-19

This Scripture is used today by HRM teachers today to convince Gentile believers they should keep the Feast of Tabernacles (as well as the other feasts). According to many HRM teachers, the Feast of Tabernacles is a dry run for the Millennium when all nations will be required to keep it. Yet, in saying that, they overlook the fact that in order to keep the Feast of Tabernacles properly, certain sacrifices had to be offered. Since there is no longer a temple, such sacrifices could not be offered, thereby nullifying the ability to keep it. That is besides the fact that such a dress rehearsal is not necessary.

If Israel already tried it and couldn't get it right, what hope is there that we will? God knew we couldn't, and that is why He sent Jesus to redeem us.

Should Gentiles Keep the Feasts?

One of the major reasons the HRM attracts many non-Jewish believers today is the appeal of keeping the Jewish feast days. I have met Gentile believers in many congregations who are convinced they should be keeping the Old Testament feast days. Like Ralph in chapter 1, they describe how much more meaningful their worship life has become by observing them. When asked for a Scriptural reason for keeping the feasts, they often point to the apostle Paul's instructions to the Corinthians to "celebrate the feast," which they interpret as a command to literally keep the Passover.

But Paul is not telling these believers (many of whom were non-Jews) to *literally* observe the Passover but to celebrate it as New Covenant believers through what is now known as the Lord's Supper. In other words, they were to see in the shadow what had already come as the Substance. Why else would the apostle allude to the Messiah as the true Passover lamb, which has been sacrificed for us? (1 Corinthians 5:7)

We should remember that immediately following the slaughter of the Passover lamb, the Israelites were commanded to keep the Feast of Unleavened Bread (Exodus 23:14-15). That feast was such an integral part of the Passover; it became subsumed into it. Once the Passover lambs were slaughtered, Israel was to remove all leaven from their homes, and for seven days, eat only unleavened bread. Paul's words to the Corinthians that they should "keep the feast" is a clear reference to the Feast of Unleavened Bread. Let's back up to include the entire paragraph:

> Your boasting is not good. Do you not know that
> a little leaven leavens the whole lump? Cleanse out
> the old leaven that you may be a new lump, as you

really are unleavened. For Christ, our Passover lamb, has been sacrificed. Let us therefore celebrate the festival, not with the old leaven, the leaven of malice and evil, but with the unleavened bread of sincerity and truth.

— 1 Corinthians 5:6-8

Paul's reference to their removing leaven pertains to removing it from their lives, not their food. ("Cleanse out the old leaven that you may be a new lump, as you really are unleavened.") That is why he refers to it as the leaven of ungodliness. They were now set apart through the Messiah's death to be unleavened (pure). So the literal observance of Passover and its elements is now interpreted in the light of the Substance, which has come in Jesus. When Paul tells them to "celebrate the feast," he is referring specifically to the Feast of Unleavened Bread. And he doesn't mean they should observe it literally but keep it by removing leaven (impurity) from their lives.

I have often asked non-Jewish believers why they feel inclined to keep the feasts. Rarely, if ever, have I had someone respond by saying, "I keep them because they are shadows that illuminate the Substance more clearly." They either say they observe them in order to be more Jewish or else to identify with the Jewish people. But few, if any, ever say they do so to enhance their knowledge of the New Covenant.

The question to ask is, "Is there any evidence that non-Jewish believers were taught by the apostles to keep the Old Testament Feasts so as to feel more Jewish or identify more closely with the Jewish people?" The answer, of course, is no. In fact, searching the New Testament thoroughly, we actually find the opposite. Why? Because teaching people, they must keep the Feasts is, in actuality, to tell them they must keep the Law. That is why the apostle Paul uses the strongest language possible to warn the Galatians they are severed from Christ if they attempt to keep the Law. In the light of this statement, everyone who keeps the feasts should search diligently what their motive for doing so is. While they are free in Christ to observe any practice they should desire, they must be careful to do it for the right reason.

Are the Christian Holidays Pagan?

One way many HRM teachers successfully convince Gentiles to keep the Jewish feasts is by persuading them the origins of Christian holidays (Christmas and Easter) are pagan. By demonizing these holidays, they are then able to present the Jewish feasts as the biblical alternative. For many HRM devotees, that fact alone (that the Christian holidays are pagan) is enough to persuade them to abandon them and begin observing the Jewish Feasts.

While there is no doubt that the origins of some Christian holidays are pagan, this is often greatly exaggerated. Theories abound about the pagan origins of Christmas trees, gift-giving, and the Winter Solstice, not to mention the fertility rites of Easter. I am not suggesting that there is no value in knowing these things. Still, what is commonly assumed to be the pagan aspects of the Christian feasts is greatly exaggerated. In fact, there is much more evidence that the three main Christian Feasts are really a Christianization of Jewish Feasts, as Daniel Juster points out:

> We should note that three of the main Christian Feasts are really a Christianization of Jewish Feasts: Passover/Pesach is celebrated as the death of Yeshua on Good Friday, Early First Fruits/Bikurim as the Resurrection, and Shavuot/Weeks

as Pentecost. Yes, the Church should connect these
Feasts much more clearly to their Jewish context.
But the assertion that the Christian versions are
pagan is painfully wrong. They celebrate the events
of prophetic fulfillment in Yeshua's life and ministry
and the day when the Holy Spirit was poured out
on the gathered disciples. The days they chose for
the actual celebrations, although different, can be
argued to be as accurate in their way as the rabbinic
dating for the feasts. These feasts celebrate Biblical
events, and we should note that the meaning is
according to what Christians have celebrated. The
origin of Christmas as the date of Yeshua's birth
is questionable at best, though argued as correct
by Messianic Jewish scholar Dr. John Fischer.
However, for pious Christians, it is the celebration
of the incarnation, not the worship of the Sun. So
also worship on Sunday is about the resurrection
of Yeshua on the first day of the week, not Sun
worship. The origin of the choice of Sunday worship
can be argued, but it has been claimed as the day of
resurrection for at least 1800 years.[1]

Consider, for example, Paul's instructions to the Corinthians
regarding eating meat offered to idols (1 Corinthians 8).
Apparently, the Corinthians had asked Paul in another letter if
believers should ever eat meat offered to idols. One would think
that Paul would immediately prohibit believers from eating such
meat since the person is aware that it has been offered to idols.
Most believers today would definitely condemn such eating.
But Paul refuses to make a law prohibiting the eating of such
meat, leaving it instead to the personal conscience of the believer.

How much easier it would have been for Paul to have set up a law condemning anyone who ate meat offered to idols. But he refuses to do so, instead—leaving it up to each man and woman's personal conscience to determine for themselves—what a marvelous testament to Paul's understanding of grace.

We should place the Christian holidays in the same light. Believers are free to observe them, even knowing that some of the practices associated with them are pagan. For example, most people who celebrate Christmas are aware that Jesus was most likely not born in December. Nevertheless, they are free to celebrate it if their conscience so allows. The same can be said of Easter. Many Christians are aware of the pagan traditions most likely imported into that holiday. The term "Easter" is itself derived from the term used by the goddess of the Anglo-Saxons named *Eostre*. While we can't deny that pagan practices became incorporated into some of these Christian holidays, believers are free to keep them as long as they are firmly convinced in their own minds. In Paul's teaching, though, he makes it clear that believers do not allow this freedom to become a stumbling block to others:

> However, not all possess this knowledge. But some, through former association with idols, eat food as really offered to an idol, and their conscience, being weak, is defiled. Food will not commend us to God. We are no worse off if we do not eat, and no better off if we do. But take care that this right of yours does not somehow become a stumbling block to the weak.[6]

> — 1 Corinthians 8:7-9

Is there a reason a believer might have to study and observe the Jewish feasts? Absolutely. Believers can be greatly helped by studying these shadows so as to understand all that has come in the Messiah. In fact, everything found in the Old Testament (including the feasts) falls into the shadow realm and is profitable for study in order to more clearly understand the New Covenant. A shadow is not the reality of a thing but a reflection of it. If I invited you to my house to eat a meal with me and all you got to see was my shadow, you wouldn't be satisfied. You want to experience my person; my shadow would never replace having fellowship with the real person.

The Hebrew Bible was the period of shadows. These elaborate shadows were given to prepare the people for the day when the reality of the Messiah would come. This is the reason for studying the Old Testament feasts. Yet many non-Jewish believers today are observing them because they believe the Christian holidays are pagan or they feel closer to God doing so. This negates the fact that the only way into the presence of God under the New Covenant is through faith in the finished work of the Messiah.

Aren't the Feasts to Be Kept Forever?

One argument made by those who teach that believers ought to keep the feasts is that God commanded that they be kept "forever." At least four places in the Old Testament, the word *forever* is used in relation to the keeping of the feasts (Exodus 12:14, 17; Leviticus 23:41; 2 Chronicles 2:4). Doesn't this indicate that the feasts are to be celebrated without end? One would think so based on the simple definition of the word forever as meaning "without end." But the truth is, forever does not always mean "without end." Let me explain.

In Exodus 21, God gives Moses instruction regarding the purchase and care of Hebrew slaves. If a man fell in debt to another Hebrew and could not pay him back, he was allowed to become a slave to that man for six years until his debt was paid. We should not think of this form of slavery in terms of what we had in America in the nineteenth century. It was more like becoming an employee rather than a cruel servitude. But if, after working off his debt for six years, he came to have affection for his master, God made a special provision by which he could serve his master forever. The provision called for that man to be brought to the door and have his ear bored through with an awl. And the result is that this man became his slave *forever* (Exodus 21:1-6).

But common sense would never interpret the word forever in the text as meaning without end for the simple reason that if the master dies, the slave can no longer serve him. The word forever is better understood as meaning *perpetual* rather than without end. Obviously, this means that this was to be observed without end so long as the factors involved continue to exist, such as the continual life of the master. If the master dies, it stands to reason that the agreement is annulled.

As demonstrated at the beginning of this chapter, Zechariah prophesied that the nations would keep the Feast of Tabernacles in the future (Zechariah 14:16-19). But that is only possible if the temple is standing (since that is the only way the sacrifices which were required for that feast could be offered). The same is true of the Passover and the seven days of Unleavened Bread immediately following it. God said,

> You shall observe the Feast of Unleavened Bread,
> for on this very day I brought your hosts out of the
> land of Egypt. Therefore you shall observe this day,
> throughout your generations, as a statute *forever.*
>
> — Exodus 12:17 (italics mine)

Notice that these things were to be celebrated *forever*. But again, once Israel came into their land of promise, they were only allowed to offer their sacrifices in the temple. So this was only possible as long as certain factors exist—namely, the continuance of the temple.

The most obvious example of this can be found in the kosher laws governing what Israel could and could not eat (Leviticus 11). While the word forever was not precisely used, God told Israel that they were to only eat clean foods as a vital part of the call to be holy (Leviticus 11:44-45). But when we come into the New Testament, we see the Messiah doing away with the kosher laws, declaring all foods clean (Mark 7:14-19). That doesn't mean that everything is best to eat for health reasons (which is a different topic altogether). It means that holiness was no longer determined by what one ate or didn't eat.

In the same way, God never intended that the Jewish feasts be outwardly observed forever. This is not because the Christian festivals have superseded them, but because they were absorbed into the Substance when the Messiah came. That is exactly what the apostle says to the Gentile church at Colosse, which was being tempted to embrace Gnostic teaching, including keeping of Jewish feast days:

> Therefore let no one pass judgment on you in questions of food and drink, or with regard to a festival or a new moon or a Sabbath. These are a shadow of the things to come, but the substance belongs to Christ.
>
> — Colossians 2:16-17

It is clear, therefore, that celebration of the feasts is not commanded in the New Testament and should not be practiced in a binding or legalistic way. Though one is free to keep the feasts if he or she chooses, there is no command that either Jewish or non-Jewish believers are obligated to keep them. They are important as shadows reflecting on the Substance—indeed, I encourage such study as a powerful means of explaining the New Covenant. In many of the churches where I have served in pastoral ministry, I have taught on the various feasts throughout the year. This has been very meaningful, especially for non-Jewish believers who have never grown up with them. I strongly encourage such teaching in churches as a means of exploring all that has come in Jesus the Messiah.

Still, it's important to underscore that the Jewish apostles never demanded that Gentiles who believe keep the feasts as a covenantal obligation. Perhaps there is no place where this is more clearly displayed than in a short letter the apostle Paul wrote to a mostly Gentile congregation. That will be the focus of the next chapter.

CHAPTER 7

All Things Loss

Philippians is one of the shortest yet most powerful of all Paul's letters. This small fellowship Paul founded on his second apostolic journey and subsequently wrote to while imprisoned in Rome was near and dear to his heart. Except for a minor scuffle between two women co-workers and some exposure to false teaching, he has mostly good things to say about them. Paul loved these saints, and it comes across in the tender language used throughout the letter.

Yet, in a letter so endearing, there is a wealth of theological acumen. In Philippians, Paul gives some of the greatest insights he gave any church when it comes to understanding personal identity in the Messiah. Not surprisingly, this is one of the most personal letters he wrote.

What's most incredible about this is that the Philippian assembly was primarily a Gentile congregation with few, if any, Jews. How do we know that? Luke tells us that when Paul and Silas came to Philippi, they found a place of prayer by the river on the Sabbath (Acts 16:13). Luke refers to it as a *proseuche,* the technical term used of buildings that were places of prayer, usually by riversides. Since it was required to have a minimum of ten male Jews thirteen years old or older (called a "minyan") in order to have a synagogue, it is safe to say that there were not even ten male Jews in Philippi. Instead, there were some women converts to Judaism that would gather for prayer by the river on the Sabbath. Among them was Lydia, whose heart God opened to listen to the things spoken by Paul (Acts 16:14-15). Lydia believed and invited Paul and the team to stay in her house.

The fact that this was a Gentile church is important in understanding not only what Paul said but what he didn't say in this letter. There is no instruction given by the apostle in this letter that these believers should keep the Law of Moses. If ever Paul wanted to make clear that he was teaching Gentile believers were responsible to keep the law, Philippi would have been the perfect place to do it. But Paul never does that anywhere in this letter. In fact, he does the opposite. As an example, look how he introduces his final exhortation to the Philippian church beginning in the third chapter:

> Look out for the dogs, look out for the evildoers,
> look out for those who mutilate the flesh. For we are
> the circumcision, who worship by the Spirit of God
> and glory in Christ Jesus and put no confidence in
> the flesh.
>
> — Philippians 3:2-3

It is important to note that Paul uses terms here that Jews originally used of Gentiles; only he used these to describe the Judaizers who were trying to get Gentile believers to be circumcised (Philippians 3:2). A Pharisee rose each morning and prayed, "I thank you Lord, that I'm not like other men. I am not a dog" (a derogatory term used of Gentiles). Paul uses it here in Philippians of those who insisted Gentile believers be circumcised. He then warns against the evildoers, another term originally used of the Gentiles. And finally, in a reference to circumcision, he speaks of those who "mutilate the flesh"

(Philippians 3:2). That Paul is definitely referring to circumcision in using that phrase is evident from the next verse: "For we are the circumcision, who worship by the Spirit of God and glory in Christ Jesus and put no confidence in the flesh" (Philippians 3:3). Here, Paul speaks of Gentile believers as the true circumcision; not a mark made in the flesh with human hands, but by the Spirit in the heart. Paul is absolutely clear that those who are truly circumcised are not those carrying a mark in their bodies, but who have had their flesh cut away by the circumcision of Christ: "In him also you were circumcised with a circumcision made without hands, by putting off the body of the flesh, by the circumcision of Christ" (Colossians 2:11).

Could anything be clearer? Gentile believers (along with their Jewish counterparts) are the *true* circumcision. Belonging to the people of God is not a matter of outward rituals such as circumcision or observing of feasts or Sabbaths, but the regenerative work of God.

Paul: The Perfect Example

In the next few verses (Colossians 3:4-6), Paul talks about the advantages he formerly had as a first-century Jew under the Law. Circumcised on the eighth day, he was a member not only of the people of Israel but of an illustrious tribe (no doubt named after Israel's first king, Saul). The reference to his being a "Hebrew of Hebrews" probably refers to his speaking only Hebrew in his home growing up. As to religious convictions, he was a Pharisee, having sat in his youth at the feet of the great rabbi, Gamaliel. That he was zealous for Judaism is evident in his considering it his duty to persecute Jews who believed in Jesus as Messiah ("as to zeal a persecutor of the church").

As to righteousness attainable under the Law, Paul considered himself blameless. That doesn't mean he actually was blameless before God "since through the law comes knowledge of sin" (Romans 3:19). It meant that as far as Judaism was concerned, Paul was righteous when it came to religious obligations of a Jew under the law.

But Paul now sees all of these benefits as one great loss when it came to knowing the Messiah:

> But whatever gain I had, I counted as loss for the sake of Christ. Indeed, I count everything as loss because of the surpassing worth of knowing Christ Jesus, my Lord. For his sake I have suffered the loss of all things and count them as rubbish, in order that I may gain Christ and be found in him, not having a righteousness of my own that comes from the law, but that which comes through faith in Christ, the righteousness from God that depends on faith—that I may know him and the power of his resurrection, and may share his sufferings, becoming like him in his death, that by any means possible I may attain the resurrection from the dead.
>
> Romans 3:7-11

In the strongest words possible, Paul now disavows all he previously thought beneficial in his former life in Judaism, considering it all to be one great loss for the sake of the Messiah. He uses the word *rubbish* to describe it when comparing it with what He now found in Messiah (the English word rubbish being a cleaned-up version of the Greek word for dung or excrement).

How does this compare with what the HRM prizes:

> The answer to this conundrum is Philippians 3: all those things such as his ethnicity are skubalon

(dung) compared with the glories of Jesus Christ.
Being united to the Messiah is Paul's new way
of being human that is far more important than
ethnicity or anything else (Galatians 3:28). What
things are skubalon in Philippians 3? Being a
Hebrew of Hebrews, being a Pharisee, being zealous
for the law, having confidence in the flesh, and
even being blamelessly righteous under the law!
See Philippians 3:2-6. For our purposes, the things
that Paul counts as skubalon are the things that
the Hebrew Roots Movement prizes above Jesus
Christ.[1]

Paul goes on to describe what he has now found in Christ: a righteousness not of his own which comes through the law, but which comes through "faith in Christ, the righteousness from God that depends on faith" (Philippians 3:9). Paul now repudiates entirely any reliance on his own works (Torah-observance) for righteousness, relying on the righteousness, which is received by faith *alone*. In other words, it is believing the promise that God made to Abraham that serves as the basis of his righteousness. He knows that apart from faith he is condemned by the Law for "the law brings wrath, but where there is no law, there is no transgression" (Romans 4:15). The righteousness he enjoys is a gift of God's grace purchased by the blood of the Son of God. It is free for Paul, but it cost God everything.

For Paul, this is the only pathway to knowing Him (Philippians 3:10). He previously thought that knowing God meant the diligent observance of the Torah. But after he met the Messiah, he knew that it was only by receiving a righteousness by faith could he cultivate the knowledge of God and the Messiah.

No Torah-Observance Taught

Reading through this letter to the Philippians, what is amazing is that nowhere did Paul ever command these Gentile believers to keep the Law. If Paul believed that Gentile believers were under obligation to keep the Law, he had the perfect opportunity to teach it here since the majority (if not all) of the believers in the church at Philippi were non-Jews. But he doesn't do that anywhere in this letter. In fact, he uses the strongest language possible to negate the notion that people can be righteous through Torah observance. He didn't mention it in the letter for the simple reason he didn't teach it! Search any of his letters, and you won't find it. For Paul, the Gospel is Jesus plus nothing.

The same is true in the Roman letter. After indicting the Gentiles for their failure to keep the Law (written on their consciences), he turns his attention to the Jew and his failure to keep it as well (Romans 2:17-28). The Jews thought that they were righteous simply because they possessed the Law. But Paul makes it clear that it is not the *possession* of the Law which makes them righteous, but *obedience* to the Law. After indicting Jews for their disobedience, he summarizes how the whole world is guilty before God:

> Now we know that whatever the law says it speaks
> to those who are under the law, so that every mouth
> may be stopped, and the whole world may be held
> accountable to God. For by works of the law, no
> human being will be justified in his sight, since
> through the law comes knowledge of sin. Now
> we know that whatever the law says it speaks to
> those who are under the law, so that every mouth
> may be stopped, and the whole world may be held
> accountable to God. For by works of the law no

human being will be justified in his sight since
through the law comes knowledge of sin.

— Romans 3:19-20

The entire world stands condemned before God because of their
failure to keep the Law. The law was never intended to be the
means of obtaining righteousness but the instrument by which
guilty sinners are convicted of their law-breaking. This is so that
they might be driven to God by faith and be justified:

But now the righteousness of God has been
manifested apart from the law, although the
Law and the Prophets bear witness to it—the
righteousness of God through faith in Jesus Christ
for all who believe. For there is no distinction: for
all have sinned and fall short of the glory of God,
and are justified by his grace as a gift, through the
redemption that is in Christ Jesus, whom God put
forward as a propitiation by his blood, to be received
by faith. This was to show God's righteousness,
because in his divine forbearance he had passed
over former sins. It was to show his righteousness
at the present time, so that he might be just and the
justifier of the one who has faith in Jesus.

— Romans 3:21-26

We have already seen in a previous chapter how Paul argued
against the false teachers who had poisoned the minds of the
Galatian believers to believe a different gospel. But in actuality,
it wasn't a different gospel since there is no other gospel than the
one Paul preached. What they were believing was a perversion of
the true Gospel (Galatians 1:6-7). And as stated previously, Paul

doesn't commend the Galatians for their being more Jewish but condemns them for deserting God (Galatians 1:6).

Perhaps the most powerful argument Paul presents that Gentiles are not required to be Torah-observant are the bold, radical statements found in the Ephesian letter. Gentiles are no longer second-class citizens but now share joint-status with Jewish believers:

> Therefore remember that at one time you Gentiles
> in the flesh, called "the uncircumcision" by what
> is called the circumcision, which is made in the
> flesh by hands—remember that you were at that
> time separated from Christ, alienated from the
> commonwealth of Israel and strangers to the
> covenants of promise, having no hope and without
> God in the world.
>
> — Ephesians 2:11-12

What a picture of hopelessness Paul paints for non-Israelites before the Messiah appeared and inaugurated the New Covenant. Words such as "separated," "alienated," and "having no hope, without God in the world" are used to vividly portray the desperate state of the Gentile world before the Messiah came. Since he appeared and reconciled men and women to God, Gentiles are now co-heirs with believing Israelites. Here is how Paul describes this blessing Gentiles now enjoy in Christ:

> But now in Christ Jesus you who once were far off
> have been brought near by the blood of Christ. For
> he himself is our peace, who has made us both one
> and has broken down in his flesh the dividing wall
> of hostility by abolishing the law of commandments

expressed in ordinances, that he might create in himself one new man in place of the two, so making peace, and might reconcile us both to God in one body through the cross, thereby killing the hostility. And he came and preached peace to you who were far off and peace to those who were near. For through him we both have access in one Spirit to the Father. So then you are no longer strangers and aliens, but you are fellow citizens with the saints and members of the household of God, built on the foundation of the apostles and prophets, Christ Jesus himself being the cornerstone, in whom the whole structure, being joined together, grows into a holy temple in the Lord In him you also are being built together into a dwelling place for God by the Spirit.

— Ephesians 2:13-22

Gentile believers should luxuriate in Paul's language describing the blessings they have now received. He tells them that those who were formerly "far off" have now been "brought near by the blood of Christ." In the strongest words possible, Paul describes how God has made "both one" (Jew and Gentile) by removing the "dividing wall of hostility"; the law of commandments expressed in ordinances." Paul's reference to the "dividing wall of hostility" refers to the wall between the Court of the Gentiles in the temple and those courts only Jews were allowed to traverse. Gentiles did so on penalty of death (verse 13).

But now, God has removed the dividing wall, making it possible for Gentiles to enter in. What has God done by abolishing the "law of commandments expressed in ordinances?" He has removed the law as the basis of the covenant by which the people of God are constituted. Since the law of commandments expressed in ordinances has been abolished, the hostility that once existed between Jew and Gentile has also been permanently abolished. With its removal, the Gentiles are now no longer "strangers and aliens" but "fellow citizens with the saints and members of the household of God" (verse 19).

The term "stranger" in the text just quoted referred to Gentiles who were not full converts to Judaism but attended the synagogue and worshipped the God of Israel. Although allowed to attend, these Gentiles were never addressed in the synagogue. But now, Paul addresses them directly by announcing they are "no longer strangers and aliens but fellow citizens with the saints and members of the household of God." That means that non-Jews who believe are given full familial rights to the household of God based on grace through faith.

Summing It Up

If Paul taught that Gentiles must observe the Law to be in right-standing with God, he missed a perfect opportunity to do so when writing to the Philippians since its membership consisted almost completely of non-Jews. But he not only doesn't do it, but he also uses the strongest language possible to renounce any reliance on the things he formerly benefitted from in Judaism (Philippians 3:2-11). This flies in the face of what many HRM teachers teach today that Gentiles must be Torah-observant to be accepted by God. The teaching of the apostle Paul, who was given a special dispensation of grace for the Gentiles, negates that in every way. The apostle clearly taught in all of his writings that Gentiles were justified the same way that their Jewish counterpart—through faith *alone*.

It is little wonder, therefore, that passages like the third chapter of Philippians are almost never referred to by teachers in the HRM. There are many other passages that HRM teachers ignore. They set forth the amazing truth that Gentile believers are now justified without attempting to keep the law.

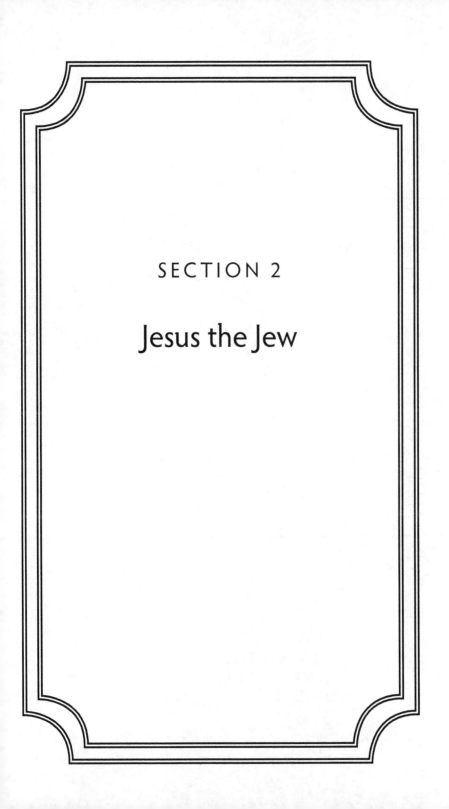

SECTION 2

Jesus the Jew

CHAPTER 8

The Jewishness of Jesus: What's in a Name

The next time you attend a Christmas service, you will most likely hear a portion of the first chapter of Matthew's Gospel read beginning with Matthew 1:18: "Now, the birth of Jesus Christ took place in this way. When his mother Mary had been betrothed to Joseph, before they came together she was found to be with child from the Holy Spirit" (Matthew 1:18).

There will primarily be a number of verses read from Luke as well. These two books tell the incredible story of how God supernaturally impregnated a young Jewish virgin to bring His Son, the Messiah, into the world. That story never gets old. It is truly the *"Greatest Story Ever Told."*

Rarely, if ever, are you likely to hear the first seventeen verses of Matthew chapter one read during a Christmas service. One reason (though few will admit it) is that the majority of readers have difficulty pronouncing many of these Hebrew names. So it's just easier to avoid them altogether and start reading in verse eighteen, which tells us how Joseph was betrothed to Mary, who turned up with Child from the Holy Spirit.

There's nothing inherently wrong with beginning the reading from there. But by doing so, the impression is given that the story of Jesus begins with Mary being impregnated while she was engaged to Joseph. But that is not where his story begins. Matthew bothers giving us a long list of names precisely because he intends to tell us where the story actually begins:

> Because says Matthew, you won't understand the
> story—the one I am about to tell you—unless you
> see it in the light of a much longer story which goes
> back for many centuries but leads up to the Jesus
> you want to know about. And that longer story is
> the history of the Hebrew Bible, or what Christians
> came to call the Old Testament. It is the story
> which Matthew "tells" in the form of a schematized
> genealogy—the ancestry of the Messiah. [1]

Matthew is telling us through Jesus' genealogy that to understand the story of Jesus, you must see it in the context of the much larger story. It is the story of the Old Testament, beginning with a man named Abraham. In other words, you cannot understand who Jesus is unless you connect him to his larger history extending back to the Old Testament:

> What Matthew is saying to us by beginning in this
> way is that we will only understand Jesus properly
> if we see him in the light of this story which he
> completes and brings to its climax. So when we
> turn the page from the Old to the New Testament,
> we find a link between the two, which is more
> important than the attention, we usually give it. It
> is a central historical interface binding together the
> two great acts of God's drama of salvation. The Old
> Testament tells the story which Jesus completes. [2]

This genealogy at the beginning of Matthew's Gospel has a lot of personal meaning for me. Prior to my conversion at seventeen, I never even held a New Testament in my hands, let alone read it. But after deciding to run away from my home in Miami and head back to my hometown of Philadelphia, I hitchhiked for three days until I came to a small town in Maryland where I was picked up by three believers late one night. After pouring my heart out to these strangers, the man in the front seat turned around and asked me, "Do you know Jesus?" Because my brother had become a believer and was in Bible school preparing for ministry, I answered, "Yes, my brother is in Bible school!" But the man was unrelenting and asked, "No, do you know Jesus?"

He then invited me to spend the night at their house and offered to buy me a bus ticket to Philadelphia the next day. That evening and into the wee hours of the morning, I sat in their living room as they shared with me the glorious Gospel. Though I had heard it before from the lips of my brother, I was blown away by the love they demonstrated for me, a total stranger. In the morning, they took me to the bus station and bought me a bus ticket to Philadelphia as promised. As I boarded the bus, I thanked them for their hospitality when one of the men reached into his pocket and handed me a small New Testament. I took it and quickly stuffed into my coat pocket as I boarded the bus and sat down.

For the entirety of the bus ride to Philadelphia, I wrestled whether to pull it out and read it. Even though I wasn't raised in a religious home, I had all of the common Jewish presuppositions regarding it. I just knew that it would prove to be the most Gentile book in the world. As a Jew, I not only had the typical ideas about the New Testament but also about who Jesus was. I knew He was Jewish, but somehow I believed that at some time in his life, He became a Catholic and went around Israel sprinkling holy water on people. That was the extent of my knowledge about Jesus.

Eventually, curiosity got the best of me and, pulling it out, I opened to the first verse of the New Testament and read these words: "The book of the genealogy of Jesus Christ, the son of *David*, the son of *Abraham*" (Matthew 1:1; italics mine).

Those words startled me; I did not expect it. It was so Jewish! Matthew begins his account by referring to the two main personages of Hebrew history I grew up with (Abraham and David). As I continued reading the genealogy of Jesus recorded in the first seventeen verses, I recognized many of the names. I was reading the history of my people in the Hebrew Bible, beginning with Abraham. (By the way, the realization that I was wrong about the Jewishness of the New Testament helped me to come to terms with the fact that perhaps I was wrong about the Messiahship of Jesus as well). A year and a half later, I came to believe that Jesus truly was the Messiah and made a full and complete commitment of my life to Him.

The Loss of the Jewishness of Jesus

It's not surprising that the very first thing we learn about Jesus from the New Testament is that He was a Jew. This is important because much of the Church world has lost connection with the *Jewish* Jesus. Years ago, I remember reading a statement from a rabbi that made a lot of sense. I can't quote it verbatim, but it was something to the effect, "Jews don't need to discover a Christian Christ as much as Christians need to discover a Jewish Jesus." While we would say emphatically that Jews *do* need to discover the truth regarding Jesus as Messiah (a Christian Christ), there is much truth in what the rabbi said. Christians need to familiarize themselves with the Jewishness of Jesus as presented in the pages of the New Testament.

The fact that Jesus was Jewish is clearly presented in the Gospels, especially the Synoptic accounts (Matthew, Mark, and Luke). He regularly attended synagogues throughout the land of Israel and taught in them frequently, especially during His Galilean campaigns (Mark 1:21, Luke 4:15). He also regularly attended the temple during His earthly ministry, observing the three feasts every male Jew was required to observe at the temple. There can be no doubt (if one looks at the evidence) that Jesus was a Jew. While most Christians acknowledge that, the greatest danger does not come from those who deny His Jewishness outright, but from Christians who are so accustomed to seeing Him from a Christian perspective, they have almost lost entirely the simple truth that He was a Jew:

> To wrench Jesus out of his Jewish world destroys
> Jesus and destroys Christianity, the religion that
> grew out of his teachings. Even Jesus' most familiar
> role as Christ is a Jewish role. If Christians leave the
> concrete realities of Jesus' life and of the history of
> Israel in favor of a mythic, universal, spiritual Jesus
> and an otherworldly kingdom of God, they deny
> their origins in Israel, their history, and the God
> who has loved and protected Israel and the church.
> They cease to interpret the actual Jesus sent by God
> and remake him in their own image and likeness.
> The dangers are obvious.[3]

Saying "Jesus was Jewish" seems so obvious it doesn't bear repeating. Still, many Christians have forgotten (or perhaps never learned) this fact. If asked before I became a believer who Jesus was, I couldn't answer in a way that would retain His Jewishness. The surprising thing is that, after entering the

Church in 1971, I quickly learned that few non-Jewish believers had an understanding of Jesus' Jewishness either. Each year I conduct a Passover Seder in which I reenact all of the events in the Upper Room in the context of the Seder meal. To this day, I have received the most powerful response to any teaching I have done. What surprises me the most is that few seem to understand that the Last Supper Jesus ate with His disciples was actually the Passover Seder meal.

Understanding Jesus, therefore, within the context of His Jewish background, benefits greatly in understanding His life and message. His parables were given in the context of a rich parabolic tradition in Judaism. Jesus also was identified as a rabbi by the peoples of His day. So there is a great benefit to understanding that Jesus was a Jew who emerged out of first-century Judaism. As stated earlier, Jesus is a man with a story, and that story began in the Hebrew Bible.

But that is not to say (as many HRM teachers do) that unless we thoroughly understand His Jewishness, we are unable to know Him. While there is a danger extricating Jesus from His proper Jewish context, there is also an equal danger presenting Jesus in such a way that He is unable to relate to Gentiles. The truth is, we cannot really know the Messiah anymore through fleshly means, as the apostle Paul told the Corinthians, "From now on, therefore, we regard no one according to the flesh. Even though we once regarded Christ according to the flesh, we regard him thus no longer" (2 Corinthians 5:16).

Paul is saying that although we once knew Jesus after the flesh, yet now we know Him no longer that way. Instead, we now know Him by the power of the Holy Spirit. That is why knowing Him as a first-century Jew, while beneficial, can't lead us to a proper assessment of His Person. *When HRM teachers focus solely on the Jewishness of Jesus, not taking into account that we no longer know Him after the flesh, they are presenting a distorted view of the*

Lord's identity. It's true that we once did know Him after the flesh, but now we no longer know Him in that fashion.

Yeshua or Jesus?

Most messianic congregations, as well as HRM teachers today, refer to the Lord by His Hebrew name, *Yeshua.* Is it wrong to use it? The simple answer is no as long as we realize that Yeshua is His Hebrew name, derived from the proper name Joshua or Yohushua, which means "Yahweh is salvation." If we were to spell it in English, it's "Joshua." That means *Joshua* and *Jesus* are the same names, one translated from Hebrew into English, the other from Greek into English.

There is no doubt that Yeshua is the Lord's real name in Hebrew, but that doesn't mean He isn't recognized by other names in other languages. Changing a word from one language to another doesn't mean we are speaking of another entity:

> In German, our English word for book is "buch."
> In Spanish, it becomes a "libro"; in French, a
> "livre." The language changes, but the object itself
> does not. In the same way, we can refer to Jesus as
> "Jesus," "Yeshua," or "YehSou" (Cantonese) without
> changing His nature. In any language, His name
> means "the Lord is Salvation." [4]

We don't call Him Yeshua if we are English speakers because that is His name in Hebrew:

> The Bible nowhere commands us to only speak or
> write His name in Hebrew or Greek. It never even
> hints at such an idea. Rather, when the message

of the Gospel was being proclaimed on the Day
of Pentecost, the apostles spoke in the languages
of the "Parthians, Medes and Elamites; residents
of Mesopotamia, Judea and Cappadocia, Pontus
and Asia, Phrygia and Pamphylia, Egypt and the
parts of Libya near Cyrene" (Acts 2:9–10). In the
power of the Holy Spirit, Jesus was made known
to every language group in a way they could readily
understand. Spelling did not matter.[5]

We refer to Him as "Jesus" because, as English-speaking
people, we know of Him through English translations of the
Greek New Testament. Scripture does not value one language
over another, and it gives no indication we must resort to Hebrew
when addressing the Lord. The command is to "call on the name
of the Lord," with the promise that we "shall be saved" (Acts
2:21; Joel 2:32). "Whether we call on Him in English, Korean,
Hindi, or Hebrew, the result is the same—the Lord is salvation."[6]

It is certainly not wrong for an English speaker to call Him
Yeshua if he or she so desires. But if one is an English speaker,
it is not wrong to call Him Jesus either, for that is the way His
name is pronounced in English. That's why Moses is the proper
way of pronouncing his Hebrew name (Moshe) in English.

Some in the HRM teach that the English name Jesus is
actually a reference to Zeus and that anyone who uses the name
Jesus is therefore offering praise to a false god. They attempt to
prove this by pointing to the fact that the second syllable of the
name Jesus (-sus) sounds similar to the Greek god Zeus. But
just because a word or part of a word sounds like another word
doesn't mean it is the same thing. The word humorous sounds
like humerus, but they don't mean the same thing at all; one

refers to being funny, while the other to the bone, which goes from the shoulder to the elbow.

In the 1930s, a movement arose out of the Church of God known as the "Sacred Name Movement." It taught that only "Yahweh" and "Yashua" were proper names for God and the Messiah. According to this movement, the use of any other name is blasphemy. The authors of both the Old and New Testaments, under the inspiration of the Holy Spirit, referred to God as Elohim (Hebrew) and Theos (Greek). So although the name will be pronounced differently in different languages, it still speaks of the same person. It is the Person that matters, not how His name is pronounced in a particular language.

Using His Hebrew Name for Evangelism

One reason many HRM teachers, as well as messianic Jews, use Jesus' Hebrew name is for evangelism. Since most non-believing Jews have an aversion to the name Jesus, they believe the Gospel will be more appealing to Jews by using His Hebrew name. There is no doubt that for many Jews, the name of Jesus is offensive, conjuring up images of crosses, church buildings, and other things associated with Gentiles and Christianity. So, it is not surprising that many desire to use His Hebrew name when sharing the Gospel with Jews. They also avoid other terms such as "New Testament," "cross," and "church," which can be repulsive to Jews. This allows Jews to hear the Gospel in a more Jewish context and cuts down on the built-in prejudices most Jews have towards Jesus.

This is in line with what the apostle Paul means when he told the Corinthian church "to the Jews, I became as a Jew, in order to win Jews" (1 Corinthians 9:20). While he would never change his Gospel to accommodate his hearers, he would change the way he presented it to suit various audiences (compare Paul's speech to the synagogue in Antioch in Acts 13 to his presenting the Gospel to Greeks at Athens in Acts 17). In a word, cultural specificity is a necessity to fulfill the apostolic mandate to bring the Gospel to the entire world.

That being said, even though we recognize the need for cultural sensitivity when presenting the Gospel to Jews, is that really what is going on when it comes to using Jesus' Hebrew name? Perhaps for some. Still, when style and cultural specificity become more important than the message itself, then we have made something more important than the Gospel. Sadly, that is exactly what is happening in much of the HRM today.

While cultural specificity is important to winning any group, no attempt to present Jesus in a Jewish context cuts down on the reality that the Jewish people have rejected Him as the Messiah. Stephen, in Acts 7, gave what can only be called a "Hebrew apologetic," defending the Gospel from the Hebrew Scriptures by presenting Jesus as the fulfillment of all the promises made to the fathers. He was not only rejected but subsequently stoned to death. Why? Because they could not bear to hear that they rejected the Messiah who was sent to them.

That is why it is bogus for Jewish believers to think that they will win their fellow Jews to faith in Jesus as the Messiah simply by demonstrating they are still Jews after believing. Since Jews do not believe one can remain Jewish and believe in Jesus, no attempts at living a Jewish lifestyle will convince those in the Jewish community otherwise. It is an exercise in futility since that will never happen, as Stan Telchin reminds us:

> This desire for acceptance, however, will not happen
> unless the Lord intervenes. Having lived my life in
> and having been part of the Jewish community for,
> lo, these many years, I am able to say to you that

Messianic Judaism will never succeed in winning acceptance by the traditional Jewish community. William Varner, Arnold Fruchtenbaum and others all agree that Messianic Jews will never be able to please Jewish religious leaders today, no matter how "Jewish" they try to be.[7]

Not surprisingly, the majority of Jews to this day still come to faith largely through Gentile witness. Hearing the Gospel from Jews who continue living a Jewish lifestyle after coming to faith figured low on all the surveys when it came to reasons Jews came to believe in Jesus as the Messiah. The truth is, unbelieving Jews are blinded to the truth of the Gospel and cannot believe until the veil is lifted off their minds (Romans 11:8, 2 Corinthians 3:14). That means there is more to their blindness to overcome than two thousand years of Christian history. The cumulative effect of centuries of unbelief can only be overturned by the working of the Spirit of God. So while we should certainly be sensitive in the way we present the Gospel to Jews, sensitivity alone will not guarantee a hearing,

Summing It Up

Jesus was born a Jew and came out of the rich background of the history of the Hebrew Bible. We have lost that emphasis in much of the church world today, as evidenced by the fact that when we talk about His beginnings, we almost always begin with the Babe in the manger. We are strangers to His greater history as a son of Abraham, a son of David (Matthew 1:1).

But we must balance this necessary biblical emphasis with the reality that we no longer know Him after the flesh (2 Corinthians 5:16). Jesus can only be known as the Spirit reveals Him. This must be taken into account when attempting to share the Gospel with Jews. While using Jesus' Hebrew name might be important when it comes to Jewish sensitivity, it alone cannot serve to make Jesus real to unbelievers. Only by the working of the Spirit of God opening Jewish minds (and for that matter everyone) can Jews be persuaded of the Messiahship of Jesus.

In the next chapter, we will examine the premiere text used by most HRM teachers to underscore the teaching that Jesus calls believers to keep the Law, even after coming to faith.

CHAPTER 9

Destroy or Fulfill

It is not surprising that the Messiah's words in the Sermon on the Mount found in Matthew 5:17 are foundational to the beliefs of the HRM. Since many teach that believers are still under the Law, a book dealing with the HRM must address this matter. Here is the text in its entirety, including the verses that follow:

> Do not think that I have come to abolish the Law
> or the Prophets; I have not come to abolish them
> but to fulfill them. For truly, I say to you, until
> heaven and earth pass away, not an iota, not a dot,
> will pass from the Law until all is accomplished.
> Therefore whoever relaxes one of the least of these
> commandments and teaches others to do the same
> will be called least in the kingdom of heaven, but
> whoever does them and teaches them will be called
> great in the kingdom of heaven. For I tell you unless
> your righteousness exceeds that of the scribes and
> Pharisees, you will never enter the kingdom of
> heaven.
>
> — Matthew 5:17-20

These verses introduce a section of the Sermon known typically as the Antithesis (Matthew 5:21-48), which contains several examples of the principle enumerated in verse 17. According to many HRM teachers, these verses clearly teach that Jesus not only kept the Law Himself, He expected His followers to as well. Many of them also quote verses such as 1 John 2:4 and 1 John 3:4 to underscore their belief that both Jesus and the apostles expected their followers to keep the Torah.

But as I will seek to demonstrate in this chapter, that is not what Jesus meant by these words. Rather, by keeping the Law Himself (the only One who ever did) and by means of His death and resurrection, He made it possible for the righteousness of the Law to be given as a gift to all those under the New Covenant. In this way, He fulfilled the Law and the Prophets. This, I believe, is the proper way to interpret these important words of Jesus.

> But that is not how many HRM adherents and teachers interpret this text. Tim Hegg, an HRM teacher, says unabashedly, "Our lives should be characterized by obedience to the Torah."[1] In another online article, Glenn McWilliams says, "I would suggest to my Christian brothers that they re-think their position on the Torah and Yeshua and repent and join us in keeping the Torah."[2]

There is no getting around it; one of the main tenets of the HRM is the belief that if followers of Jesus want to be godly, they are obligated to keep the Torah.

The Hebrew Roots Movement and Torah

In the opening paragraph of the article previously quoted, Glenn McWilliams says the following:

> For centuries the Church has been teaching unsuspecting believers that Jesus came to set them free from the Law of YHWH ELOHIM. This has led many sincere Christians to believe that it is alright for them to live contrary to the very clear teaching of the scriptures. The Torah clearly teaches that the Sabbath is YHWH'S set apart day. The Torah clearly teaches that we are not to work on the Sabbath nor are we to cause any one else to work on the Sabbath. The Torah clearly states that the Sabbath is the seventh day of the week. Yet the Church teaches that we do not have to keep the Sabbath on the seventh day, that we do have to abstain from working on the Sabbath, nor is their anything wrong with believers causing other people to work of the Sabbath to accommodate our worldly dining and shopping habits. We do not have to follow the very clear instructions of the Torah because Jesus came to fulfill the Law and therefore did away with it. Therefore, according to the Church, even though the Eternal One commanded it, bound himself by it, had the people of Israel agree to it, had Moses record it, and sent his Son Yeshua to teach it and live it out before us, we are no longer obligated to do it. The Church erroneously teaches that because Jesus fulfilled the Law we are no longer obligated to keep YHWH'S Law. It is no wonder that the Jews have rejected the Church, Christianity,

and their Jesus. The idea that the Messiah would come and free people from the Torah is contrary to every word about the Messiah found in the scriptures! Beyond this there is a great hypocrisy evident in the teaching of the Church.[3]

In the remainder of the article, he condemns the Church for what he sees as its hypocrisy. While teaching people they are no longer obligated to observe things like the feasts or dietary laws; they demand that they still obey the moral commandments such as ceasing from adultery, stealing, and lying. He then mocks the Church's teaching that there were two aspects to the Law; the moral law and the ritual law, and that Jesus came only to do away with the ritual Law. For McWilliams and others like him, the Torah (Law) is still binding upon believers, whether Jewish or Gentile.

There is no doubt that the Torah was the foundation for Jews under the Old Covenant, containing the six hundred thirteen laws every Jew was required to keep. Given by God to Moses on Mount Sinai, these laws governed Israel's entire existence. For Jews, therefore, the "Torah serves as the foundation to all subsequent understanding and interpretation of Scripture" (Wikipedia, Hebrew Roots). HRM adherents, as well as messianic Jews, hold to the same view that the Torah is the foundation of everything. While most agree that Jesus came to redeem them from the penalty of broken Law, He did so that all who believe might live a life of obedience to Torah. Indeed, the majority of HRM adherents today are Gentiles who testify to the blessing of living a Torah observant life. According to Paul Nison, this is due to the universal nature of the Torah:

The reality is the Torah was never meant for only one specific ethnic group, religion, race, creed or other distinction. It was given by the Creator of the universe that ALL people who want to seek His ways would have an illuminated path. The word Torah" itself has been mislabeled as the word "law" for centuries, but the word has much more meaning than just that. A more simple and better understanding would be guidelines or instructions.[4]

For many in the HRM, this is what John meant in Revelation when he speaks of "those who keep the commandments of God and hold to the testimony of Jesus" (Revelation 12:17). In fact, according to many HRM teachers, all New Testament references to keeping the "commandments of God," which Yeshua and His apostles spoke, refers to living a "Torah observant life." Since Jesus and His apostles commanded their followers to keep the Law, we must do the same. This is based on Jesus' own words quoted earlier in this chapter—that He did not come to "abolish the Law and the Prophets, but to fulfill" (Matthew 5:17). According to many HRM teachers and adherents, the Church abolishes the Law and the Prophets when it teaches that since Jesus came, died, and rose from the dead, believers are no longer obligated to keep the law.

What Does "Fulfill" Mean?

The key to determining what Jesus meant by His statement that He did not come to "abolish the Law and the Prophets, but to fulfill" revolves around the meaning of the word *fulfill*. Only by properly understanding that word in this sentence can we even begin to understand the meaning of His statement. We will see it either as a reinforcement of the idea largely found in HRM/Messianic Judaism, that Jews and Gentiles are obligated as believers to live Torah obedient lives. Or else, we will interpret it in the context of the righteousness which the Messiah makes possible by His living a life of perfect obedience to the Law and the Prophets and dying to expiate sin on behalf of His people.

The first thing we should note is that Jesus spoke this way precisely because many in Israel, having heard His teaching, thought that was exactly what He came to do. His teaching was so different from that which they were accustomed to in Judaism; it seemed as if He was wanting to undo it. So these words were spoken so as to make clear that far from abolishing the Law and the Prophets, He actually came to fulfill them. What exactly did He mean by *fulfill* in the statement? It could mean that He perfectly kept the Law as a Torah observant Jew. While that is certainly true, it is doubtful that is what is meant since the word *fulfill* points to His *teaching*, not to His actions. Others point to the fact that He may mean nothing more than that He completes it in the sense of revealing its true intentions. That also is true, but Matthew uses the term differently than simply to say that He came to explain the Law.

The easiest way to understand what Jesus meant by "fulfill" is by looking at how Matthew uses that term in the first four chapters of his Gospel (Matthew 1:22-23, 2:4-6, 2:15, 2:17, 3:3, 4:12-16). What is meant by its usage in these passages?

> Beginning in the first chapter of his Gospel, Matthew has taken great pains to point to Jesus as the Christ, who came in fulfillment of Old Testament prophecy. Jesus did not descend from heaven unannounced to a people who had no inkling of His appearance. No! For Matthew,

the birth and early life of Christ were predicted
centuries before His arrival, and when He appeared,
He fulfilled all that was spoken of Him.[5]

Do you see what he means? Jesus is saying that He fulfilled the
Law and the Prophets in that they predicted His coming:

> Notice that Matthew has been laying the
> foundation for this fulfillment theme throughout
> the first four chapters, so when Jesus says He came
> to fulfill, Matthew wants us to understand the
> statement in light of what has come before. That
> is to say that the Law and the Prophets pointed to
> Him prophetically. So how could people think that
> He came to get rid of the Law and the Prophets?
> They point to Christ, and Jesus is aware that His
> ministry fulfills all that was spoken before.[6]

This means that the Law and the Prophets were prophetic,
pointing to the Messiah who was to come. Apparently, Jesus
Himself understood them that way as He made clear to His
apostles in the Upper Room:

> Then he said to them, "These are my words that
> I spoke to you while I was still with you, that
> everything written about me in the Law of Moses
> and the Prophets and the Psalms must be fulfilled."
> Then he opened their minds to understand the
> Scriptures, and said to them, "Thus it is written, that
> the Christ should suffer and on the third day rise
> from the dead, and that repentance and forgiveness

of sins should be proclaimed in his name to all
nations, beginning from Jerusalem."

                                        — Luke 24:44-47

Perhaps the best way to understand this is by turning the
word "fulfill" around so as to say that Jesus not only came to
fulfill certain predictions but "fill full" the entire Tenach (Old
Testament). In other words, His coming brings out a fullness to
all Old Testament history. So while it is true that He came to
fulfill certain predictions, it is also true to say that His Coming
"fills full" the entire Bible.

The four-times Matthew uses the word fulfill in the first
four chapters of his Gospel helps to clarify this. The first time in
chapter one refers to how Messiah fulfilled the ancient prophecy
regarding the Messiah's birth at Bethlehem (Matthew 1:22-23).
There, it seems to be a straightforward use of the term; Isaiah
predicted that a virgin would conceive and bear a Son who
would be born in Bethlehem, and it happened as predicted. The
same is true in the second chapter as well; Herod inquired of the
chief priests and scribes as to where Messiah was to be born, and
they answered him from the prophecy of Micah (Micah 5:2).
These are straightforward examples of predictions made that
were literally fulfilled historically.

But they are followed by two examples that don't fit the
typical pattern of literal predictions that were fulfilled. Matthew
2:16-18 records Herod's reprisal against the male children
of Bethlehem two years and younger after realizing he had
been deceived by the wise men. Verse 17 states that Herod's
murderous rage fulfilled the ancient prophecy given through
Jeremiah in Jeremiah 31:15. But if you read the context of
that prophecy in Jeremiah, it most likely refers to the sorrow
of mothers as their children were being deported to Babylon.

How then can Matthew say that the slaughter of the Bethlehem children fulfilled what was spoken by the prophet Jeremiah? The reason Matthew can do that with this passage is simple: *He is not saying that the slaughter at Bethlehem fulfilled a particular prediction made by Jeremiah, but that it "filled full" the previous mourning of Bethlehem with new meaning.* The prophecy, if you read it in Jeremiah, focuses on Rachel, the mother of Joseph and Benjamin, and the sorrow she had giving birth to Benjamin at Bethlehem (see Genesis 35:16-20). It became a place of sorrow since Rachel died after delivering her son. Matthew says that the sorrow caused by the slaughter of Bethlehem's children is greater than the sorrow the Babylonian Captivity caused.

The same is true of Matthew's account of the departure of the Messiah from the land of Israel to Egypt in Matthew 2:13-15. Joseph was instructed to take the Child to Egypt to avoid Herod slaughtering Him, which, as we have seen, took place at Bethlehem. After Joseph took Mary and the Child to Egypt, he remained there till Herod died, as the angel told him. Matthew says this fulfilled the prophecy Hosea gave in Hosea 11:1: "When Israel was a child, I loved him, and out of Egypt, I called my son" (Hosea 11:1). But looking at it in its context, we can see that Hosea's statement isn't referring to the Messiah leaving Egypt as a Child, but the children of Israel leaving Egypt during the Exodus. How then can Matthew say the Messiah leaving Egypt as a Child fulfilled that prophecy? It's because Matthew isn't saying that Jesus leaving Egypt with His father and mother fulfills the prediction Hosea gave, but that He (Jesus) gives richer meaning to the original Exodus. In other words, He now "fills full" the original prediction by giving it a richer, more poignant meaning.

Till All Is Fulfilled

Jesus follows His statement in Matthew 5:17 that He didn't come to abolish the Law and the Prophets but to fulfill them with some other words, making it even clearer (Matthew 5:18-20). His purpose in speaking these words is to uphold the Law and the Prophets as authoritative and binding until they are fulfilled. So assured is He of this (that the Law and the Prophets are authoritative and binding until the Messiah comes) that He uses hyperbole (intended exaggeration for the sake of emphasis) to make His point. Not even a dot or an iota (the smallest letters of the Hebrew alphabet and the smallest portion of a letter) will be removed before it is fulfilled:

> And so, Jesus is going to the most extreme extent possible to tell us that nothing of God's law will pass away until all of it is fulfilled - not one single jot, and not one single tittle. We might put it this way; "Till heaven and earth pass away, not one dot of a single 'i' or one cross of a single 't' will fail from God's written law until all of it is fulfilled." Everything will happen just as God has said it will happen. When heaven and earth itself have finally passed away, it will be known to all that not a single word that the Lord had spoken will have failed (Joshua 21:45), and that all He said will have come to pass (Joshua 23:14).[5]

In verse 18, a keyword emerges; the word "until." In using this word, Jesus is saying in this statement that the Law and the Prophets were authoritative *until* the time of their fulfillment. What time frame was Jesus referring to? The simple answer is, the Law and the Prophets were in effect until the Messiah came, at which time He inaugurated a New Covenant. That covenant fulfilled all that was contained in the Law and the Prophets. There are at least three ways Scripture speaks of in regards to how He fulfilled the Law and the Prophets.

First, there are definite prophecies in the first five books that Jesus fulfilled by His appearing (Genesis 3:15, 49:10; Numbers 24:17; Deuteronomy 18:18). The first one, known as the *Protoevangelium*, is often viewed as the fountainhead of all prophecy (Genesis 3:15). There are said to be over three hundred specific predictions made in the Old Testament of the coming of Messiah, which Jesus fulfilled.

Secondly, Jesus fulfilled the *symbolic* and *ritualistic* aspects of the Law, specifically, the sacrificial system, which pointed to His atoning death. All of these sacrifices ordered under the Law were based on the simple truth stated in Leviticus 17:11: "For the life of the flesh is in the blood, and I have given it for you on the altar to make atonement for your souls, for it is the blood that makes atonement by the life" (Leviticus 17:11). The New Testament book of Hebrews was largely written to unpack how the Levitical system was fulfilled in the sacrificial death of the Jewish Messiah whose blood inaugurated a New Covenant.

But there is a third way that is often overlooked. The teaching function of the Law also points to Christ's teaching ministry. Notice what Matthew says at the end of the Sermon on the Mount—that after hearing Him teach, the people were "astonished at His teaching" (Matthew 7:28). Throughout the Sermon, Jesus appeals to His own authority rather than the authority of the Law. He is the One who speaks the words of God. In many respects, the scene of the Sermon on the Mount was prefigured by the events at Sinai. There, Moses went up to the mount, received the commandments, came down, and taught Israel. In the same way, Jesus Messiah went up to the mountain and called to Himself those who were His disciples, and they came to Him and heard His teaching.

A Righteousness that Exceeds

Jesus then adds this in His teaching:

> Therefore whoever relaxes one of the least of these commandments and teaches others to do the same will be called least in the kingdom of heaven, but whoever does them and teaches them will be called great in the kingdom of heaven. For I tell you, unless your righteousness exceeds that of the scribes and Pharisees, you will never enter the kingdom of heaven.
>
> — Matthew 5:19-20

At first glance, it would seem that Jesus is teaching that Torah observance is necessary for righteousness. But that is not at all what He is doing in this passage. Rather, He is warning about our attitude towards the commandments:

> What is Jesus doing here? Is He taking us back to some kind of obedience to the Law as a means of salvation? No! But He is focusing His lens on the connection between faithful, heartfelt obedience and those who assume they will have a position in the kingdom because of their own home-made, self-justifying righteousness.[5]

The little word *for* connecting verse nineteen to twenty is very important. It both summarizes what he has said up till now, as

well as introduces us to the Antithesis (Matthew 5:21-48). It
reveals that only a righteousness from deep within is acceptable
to God:

> If His disciples believed that they could earn a
> place in the kingdom by legalistic, self-justification,
> instead of with heartfelt obedience to God, they
> were wrong. That attitude has no part in the
> kingdom. Instead, kingdom righteousness requires
> what the Law itself required. It requires heartfelt
> obedience characterized by the love of God.[5]

When Jews in the first century thought of righteous people,
they always thought of the scribes and Pharisees. How then was
it possible for His disciples to have a righteousness that exceeded
them? As we will see, Jesus doesn't mean they are to have a
righteousness that is *quantitatively* greater but *qualitatively*
better. It would not mean a greater amount of outward deeds
which enabled them to have a righteousness exceeding that of
the scribes and Pharisees, but a righteousness springing from
within, from a changed heart.

Jesus followed these statements by giving examples of what
that righteousness looked like (Matthew 5:21-48). In describing
these things, He was simply stating the true intention of the
Law. The scribes and Pharisees were externalists who reduced
the Law to mere outward observances. For example, as long as
one didn't commit the act of adultery itself, they were considered
as having obeyed the commandment. But Jesus makes it
clear that it was not merely the act itself but the thought and
intent of the heart that mattered when it came to obeying this
commandment (Matthew 5:27-30). The same was true with the
commandment not to murder (Matthew 5:21-26). As long as

one obeyed it outwardly, he or she was considered obedient. But Jesus broadened the command to include hatred of any kind. Murder was not merely the act but the thought and intent of the heart.

The Myth of Torah Observance

The view the HRM holds that Jesus taught that believers should live Torah-observant lives flies in the face of what the New Testament has to say about the Law and the reason God gave it. The New Testament writers all agree that "the Law is holy, righteous and good" (Romans 7:12). The problem, therefore, is not with the Law at all. As the apostle reminds the Galatian believers, it was given four hundred years after the previous covenant God made with Abraham. "Why then the law? *It was added because of transgressions*, until the offspring should come to whom the promise had been made, and it was put in place through angels by an intermediary" (Galatians 3:19; italics mine). What does Paul mean by the phrase the law was added: "because of transgressions?" It means that the main purpose of the law was to expose the true nature of sin so as to prepare those under the New Covenant to receive the grace which would come through Jesus Christ.

The apostle Paul tells his young son in the faith, Timothy, the reason the Law was given:

> Certain persons, by swerving from these, have
> wandered away into vain discussion, desiring to be
> teachers of the law, without understanding either
> what they are saying or the things about which they
> make confident assertions. Now we know that the
> law is good, if one uses it lawfully, understanding
> this, that the law is not laid down for the just but

for the lawless and disobedient, for the ungodly and sinners, for the unholy and profane, for those who strike their fathers and mothers, for murderers, the sexually immoral, men who practice homosexuality, enslavers, liars, perjurers, and whatever else is contrary to sound doctrine in accordance with the gospel of the glory of the blessed God with which I have been entrusted.

— 1 Timothy 1:6-11

It was for such teaching regarding the Law that the apostle Paul was so vehemently opposed and hated during his lifetime. Even today, many in the HRM despise him and treat him and his teaching with disdain. Many HRM teachers believe that Paul created doctrines like the deity of Christ, thus creating the religion of Christendom. We will examine this more fully in the next chapter.

CHAPTER 10

Did Paul Invent Christianity?

Although we have focused primarily in this section on the Jewishness of Jesus, it will be helpful here to take a slight digression in order to examine the teaching of the apostle Paul. Since his teaching fills three-fourths of the New Testament, a good grasp on what this former Pharisee believed and wrote about Jesus is essential if we are to have a proper understanding of the New Covenant.

It goes without saying that the apostle Paul is one of the most controversial figures in the history of religion, both hated and loved by many. To those who believe that Jesus is the Jewish Messiah, he is the cherished spokesman of the faith. Where would we be without those wonderful letters he penned giving us a rationale for our faith? Not only are they essential for setting forth basic Christian beliefs, but for modeling what normative Christian living looks like as well. His life serves as the ultimate example of what it means to be a follower of the crucified Messiah.

But that same Paul, while beloved by many, is also despised, especially by those who reject Jesus as the Messiah. They consider him to be the founder of the religion of Christianity, which (according to them) Jesus never intended to start. While they believe Jesus' teaching falls within the main tenets of first-century Judaism, they blame Paul for changing his teaching. This is especially the case when it comes to Paul's teaching regarding Jesus' deity. In other words, they blame Paul for turning Jesus from a simple first-century rabbi to God Himself.

Deity of Jesus in the Gospels

Most Jews reject the clear Testament teaching that Jesus of Nazareth was God in the flesh, a key doctrine of orthodox Christianity. In fact, many Jews believe that Jesus Himself, in His teaching, never claimed to be God. Rather, they believe the apostle Paul deified Him. While many HRM devotees hold to the full deity of Jesus of Nazareth, many others agree with those who attribute this doctrine to the apostle Paul himself.

But one simply needs to turn to the four Gospels themselves to realize that Paul did not invent this doctrine but received it from Jesus Himself, who clearly taught it during His earthly ministry. On more than one occasion, Jesus not only claimed to be one with God, those who heard Him actually understood Him to claim that. There are two places in John's Gospel where this occurs. The first is in John chapter eight, which records a conversation Jesus had with Jewish leaders regarding their relationship to Abraham. Though claiming to be the children of their father Abraham, Jesus indicted them for their failure to live like Abraham (John 8:39-41). Then he startles them by making the statement, "Truly, truly, I say to you, if anyone keeps my word, he will never see death" (John 8:51). Hearing this, they reiterated their belief that he is demon-possessed (John 8:52). Abraham died, and the prophets died, yet Jesus is claiming that anyone who keeps His word will never see death. The Jewish leaders then point to the fact that their forefather Abraham, as well as the Prophets, had died—how then can Jesus claim whoever keeps His word will never see death? But Jesus only makes matters worse by claiming to exist before Abraham: Jesus said to them, "Truly, truly, I say to you, before Abraham was, I am" (John 8:58).

That they understood Him to be claiming to be a deity by this statement is obvious from their reaction: "So they picked up stones to throw at him, but Jesus hid himself and went out of the temple" (John 8:59).

The second time Jesus claimed to be deity in John's Gospel occurred at the Feast of Dedication (John 10:22-23). It was winter, and Jesus was walking in the temple when He began to be questioned again by Jewish leaders. In that exchange, He made the incredible claim, "I and the Father are one" (John 10:30). That there is no doubt they understood what he was saying is evident in that they picked up stones again to stone him (John 10:31). Jesus responded by asking, "I have shown you many good works from the Father; for which of them are you going to stone me?" Look at how they responded: "The Jews answered him, 'It is not for a good work that we are going to stone you but for blasphemy, because you, being a man, make yourself God'" (John 10:32-34).

These two passages from John substantiate Jesus' claim to be God. To deny this is to deny the veracity of Scripture. To claim that Jesus, Himself, never taught this doctrine but was invented by the apostle Paul cannot be substantiated by Scripture. Jesus fully claimed to be the Eternal One, existing before Abraham and, therefore, one with the Father.

Another place in John's Gospel where Jesus' deity is clearly taught is the twelfth chapter. John quotes from two places in the prophet Isaiah (Isaiah 53 and Isaiah 6) to account for Jewish unbelief (John 12:36-41). Let's briefly look at the stunning statement John makes after quoting from Isaiah 6:10 (John 12:40): After quoting that verse from Isaiah 6, John makes this statement: "Isaiah said these things because he saw *his* glory and spoke of Him" (John 12:41; italics mine).

This is undoubtedly a reference to the vision of the glory of God, which Isaiah saw and is recorded in the sixth chapter of his book. It is considered to be the preeminent vision of the Holy One in all of Scripture, often referred to as the "Vision of the Thrice Holy One." But who exactly did Isaiah see in this vision? John makes it clear when he says that "Isaiah said these things because he saw *his* glory and spoke of him" that it was none other than the Pre-Incarnate Messiah of Israel, the Son of God Isaiah saw in his vision.

How then can it be said that Paul invented the idea that Jesus was the very God of gods in lieu of these accounts in the Gospel of John? They establish clearly that the deity of Christ was not an idea the apostle himself created but the clear teaching of Jesus Himself.

Did Paul Invent Christianity?

Along with the claim that the apostle Paul is responsible for the deification of Jesus of Nazareth is the equal claim that Paul invented a separate religion called *Christianity*. This can be refuted on many levels. As we saw in a previous chapter, it was inevitable that the Church became separate from Judaism due to the rejection of Jesus as the Messiah by the Jewish people. At first, Jewish believers sought to remain within the mainstream of Judaism, worshipping in the synagogue as well as in the temple (Acts 2:46, Acts 5:12). This was according to divine plan since the Gospel needed to come to the "Jew first" before going to the Gentile world (Romans 1:16).

But God's plan was not limited to Israel and the Jewish people. Eventually, the Gospel would be preached among the nations, thus fulfilling the word spoken to Abraham that "in him, all the nations of the earth would be blessed" (Genesis 12:3).

This meant that it would not long remain a "temple-centered" religion.

It is clear from the book of Acts that, at first, the Jewish apostles had little understanding of the universal scope of the Gospel. But Stephen, one of the seven chosen to serve the Jerusalem widows, seems to have understood from Hebrew history that Israel had always encountered God outside of the temple (Acts 7). Whether it be Abraham to whom the divine call came to leave Chaldea and go to a land God would show him, or Moses, to whom God revealed Himself in a burning bush, these revelations were all made *apart* from the temple. Stephen's sermon was a defense against that charge he was speaking against the temple and changing the laws God had given Moses. Stephen refuted that charge, proving from Hebrew history that God constantly revealed Himself to the fathers outside of the temple.

The death of Stephen signified a major breach between Judaism and Jews who believed in Jesus. Jewish believers understood that in Jesus, Hebrew history had now found its fulfillment, thus opening the way for Gentile evangelism (Acts 11:19-22). The Gospel began to make its way westward after the stoning of Stephen through the instrumentality of the apostle Paul whose conversion on the way to Damascus was previously recorded by Luke (Acts 9:1-19). Paul was not only the agent through which the expansion of the kingdom among the Gentiles occurred but the vessel to whom was given a unique understanding of what before had only remained a mystery. Now, both Jew and Gentile were united in one body, thus forming out of two, "one new man" (Ephesians 2:11-22). This was practically demonstrated by the planting of various congregations throughout the Empire where both Jew and Gentile worshipped the living God together without requiring Gentiles to first become Jews. This battle for full acceptance of the Gentiles through the Gospel was a fight Paul would be engaged in till his dying day.

Far from inventing a new religion, therefore, Paul claimed to have spoken nothing but what the Law and the Prophets had predicted (Acts 24:14-15). If Jesus as the Messiah fulfilled all that the Law and the Prophets had foretold, then Paul remains within the mainstream of biblical Hebraism (although not within the framework of rabbinic Judaism):

> The idea that Paul invented Christianity out of some theological vacuum is completely without merit. Although Paul's Letter to the Romans is radically different from just about any other book of the Bible, the teachings found in the Book of Romans is also found in the Old Testament, the teachings of Jesus, and the teachings of the disciples. So, Paul didn't just make up doctrines to create a new religion. However, he did write the greatest theological treatise of all time in the Book of Romans. Not only are the core doctrines of Christianity found outside Paul's writings, but Paul himself taught many other theological issues that reflect the teachings of Jesus during His years of ministry. Contrary to the claims of some, Paul did not just write about some "cosmic Jesus," but described Jesus as a real man who lived and died on planet earth. In conclusion, Paul of Tarsus did not invent Christianity, but clarified the teachings of the Bible as no other Bible author ever has. In addition to his great theological writings, Paul was Christianity's greatest evangelist.[1]

Looking Ahead

We have seen in this chapter that Paul did not go beyond the teaching of Jesus Himself when it came to His claim of deity. During His earthly life and ministry, Jesus made it abundantly clear that He was God in the flesh. Nor did Paul invent a new religion, ignoring what Jesus taught in the Sermon on the Mount. Nowhere is there evidence that Paul either ignored the teaching of Jesus or denigrated it. On the contrary, he upholds the teaching of Jesus, bringing forth that further truth Jesus promised His disciples, which they could not yet receive while they were still with Him on earth (John 16:12-13). While we must acknowledge that much of what Paul had written was admittedly hard to understand (2 Peter 3:15-16), it was through this man that God gave a further understanding of the "one new man" created by Christ's life, death, and resurrection, whereby both Jew and Gentile are constituted a new humanity.

As we have seen, the theology of the "one new man" was to be displayed in local congregations, thus demonstrating a unique kingdom culture. That being the case, we should ask ourselves some important questions: If this is so, why does the HRM place ultimate emphasis on the importance of being outwardly Jewish? And why are most participants in the HRM non-Jews? And why is there more excitement about being outwardly Jewish than in knowing the Messiah?

And one very important question: Why are many Gentiles in the HRM being told that their Hebrew Roots are to be found not in biblical Hebraism but in rabbinic Judaism? We will attempt to answer these questions in the first two chapters of the next section—"Hebraic Roots or Jewish Roots?"

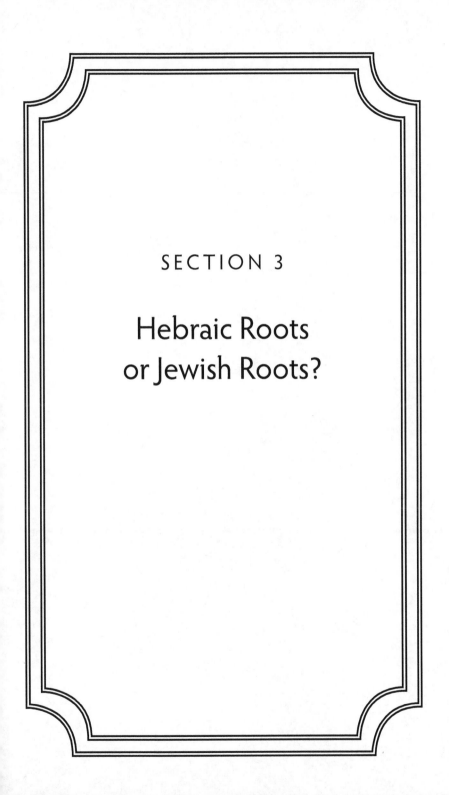

SECTION 3

Hebraic Roots
or Jewish Roots?

CHAPTER 11

For the Sake of Tradition

In this section of this book, I deal with two important issues essential to understanding the HRM. In this chapter, we look at the failure to distinguish between *biblical* Hebraic roots and *rabbinic* roots, that is, deriving our beliefs either from rabbinic tradition or from the Word of God. The chapter which follows attempts to answer the question: What is the appeal to Gentiles to join this movement?

Both chapters deal essentially with the issue of *identity*—determining who the people of God are and on what basis they have come to belong to Him. I make the case in both these chapters that the true people of God are not those living a Jewish lifestyle but those who are part of the "one new man" spoken of in Ephesians 2:15. But beyond identity, these chapters raise a fundamental question: What is the basis by which we determine truth: *tradition* or the *Word of God*? This question needs to be asked since many in the HRM are being taught to practice rabbinic Judaism under the guise of being reconciled to the Jewish roots of their faith. In other words, there is a failure to make a distinction between the traditions of Judaism, which rejected Jesus as the Messiah, and biblical Hebraism.

Yet there is a huge difference between the two, differences highlighted by the Messiah Himself during His earthly ministry. For example, the Synoptics (Matthew, Mark, Luke) record how

Jewish leaders saw Jesus' disciples eating with unwashed hands and accused them of not walking "according to the tradition of the elders, but eat with defiled hands" (Mark 7:5). In their minds, a violation of this Jewish tradition was as important (if not more important) than a violation of Scripture itself. But Jesus quoted from the twenty-ninth chapter of Isaiah where the prophet tells the Jewish leaders of his day that they "honored God with their lips while their hearts were far from him" and "worshipped him in vain, teaching as doctrines the commandments of men" (Mark 7:6-7). Clearly distinguishing between human tradition and Scripture, He chided them for allowing human tradition to take precedence over Scripture, accusing them of having "left the commandment of God in order to hold to the tradition of men" (Mark 7:8).

This is not just an ancient problem, but one that reflects on the core issues lying at the heart of the HRM today. Any movement (HRM or any other) must honestly answer the question: What is the ultimate authority upon which we base our teaching: human tradition or Scripture? I will make the case in this chapter that much of the HRM is built upon rabbinic traditions rather than the Word of God.

What Is Rabbinic Judaism?

To grasp the significance of this, it is crucial that we first have an understanding of what rabbinic Judaism is and how it emerged historically. The Judaism practiced today is radically different from that known in the Bible in that it largely emerged after the destruction of the second Temple in Jerusalem in AD 70. The changes to Judaism in the light of that event were major. The sudden loss of the center of Jewish life for Jews worldwide (the temple) was devastating. Judaism, which had previously been temple-centered, was now centered around the teaching and writings of the rabbis.

The main change was the emergence of the so-called "Oral" Law. It was built on the belief that God revealed His Torah in two parts, written and oral. What is the oral law, and when did it originate?

> Many people think that the Oral Torah was given to Moses on Mount Sinai. Many rabbis preach this view despite it being untrue to encourage Jews to obey the Oral Torah teachings believing that God ordered them to do so. Actually, the Oral Torah was developed by the Pharisees and later rabbis. The Pharisees made these adaptations before 70 CE when the rabbinical period began, and the rabbis continued the practice, which created rabbinical Judaism.[1]

Rabbinic Judaism is derived from documents created after the Temple was destroyed; the Mishnah (AD 200) and the two Talmuds, one produced in Babylon about AD 500 and the other in the land of Israel a century before: "Rabbinic Judaism, then, is the worldview way of life applied to the Jewish nation by rabbis. The Judaism under discussion is called 'Talmudic,' after its principle literary documents."[2]

The main thing to grasp regarding the change in Judaism had to do with the synagogue replacing the temple:

> Jewish religious expression was decentralized. It no longer required geography. It no longer required one temple on one mountain in one city. You can do it anywhere. The exclusivity of a temple was

replaced by the synagogues, that could now function as minor sanctuaries. It is interesting because, ultimately, Jews would talk about synagogues as assuming status of sacred space. In many ways, the synagogue does become a new expression of what was once a temple.[3]

The rabbi now emerged as the main teacher of the Torah. The word itself means "master" and is really the designation of a sage, a teacher of Torah. The restructuring of Jewish religious expression after the destruction of the temple in many ways can be defined as a sort of spiritualizing process in which the rabbis were the main motivators. Whereas in the first century, the rabbi was more of an itinerant teacher who went about teaching the Torah, the rabbi became much more institutionalized in the emergence of the synagogue after the temple was destroyed.

Rabbinic Judaism gained prominence between the 2nd and 6th centuries with the development of the Oral law and the Talmud. With the destruction of the Temple, Judaism was now faced with the question of how to function without it. Many questions remained, such as how atonement can be achieved without a temple and how to connect present and past traditions. The Council of Jamnia in AD 90 was assembled to answer these and other questions as well as determine such things as the finalization of the canon of the Hebrew Bible.

But it is also believed to be where the Jewish authorities decided to exclude believers in Jesus from synagogue attendance as referenced by interpretations of John 9:34 in the New Testament. Already, Judaism had determined that anyone who believes that Jesus is the Messiah should be put out of the synagogue, no longer recognized as a Jew.

Rabbinic Judaism and
Hebrew Roots Movement

What is shocking today is that many HRM teachers are actually advocating a return to Rabbinic, synagogue Judaism. This is amazing, especially in light of the fact that Rabbinic Judaism rejects the Messiah to this day. Nevertheless, many HRM teachers continue to teach things that are not in the Word of God but are Talmudic traditions, as Richard Fisher makes clear:

> It is obvious in much of the HRM that it's not just
> the study of the first century for interpretation,
> information, and illumination that carries the day
> but keeping the traditions and practices of the
> Jewish Talmud, which was completed long after
> Jesus in the years 400-500. Actually, there are two
> Talmuds, namely the Babylonian Talmud and the
> Palestinian Talmud. The Talmuds vary in many of
> their customs, traditions, and practices.[4]

What is most amazing is that many of these things being taught in the HRM are being taught largely by Gentiles. I address why the HRM is comprised almost completely of Gentiles in the next chapter. Suffice it to say, the imposition of these things upon non-Jews is dangerous:

> This imposition of Jewish practice on non-Jewish
> believers really does constitute a serious issue
> that promotes elitism, unnecessary division, wide
> confusion, and unbiblical practices. We can almost
> understand Jews who convert to Christ, who still try
> to keep some of the cultural aspects and celebrations

of their familial heritage. If their intentions and motives are not legalistic, and if these things are not done for salvation or out of religious elitism, there may be some minor benefit. Yet to impose them on Gentiles (as is the case, more often than not) is a direct violation of Paul's words to the Colossians: "So let no one judge you in food or drink, or regarding a festival or a new moon or Sabbaths, which are a shadow of things to come, but the substance is of Christ.[5]

While advocating a return to Judaism as the true root of Christianity, the HRM is ignoring the basic question: *which* Judaism? There were several different types of Judaism practiced in the first century, such as Pharasiasm (with its two schools of Shammai and Hillel) and Sadduceeism, with its liberal bent. There were also the Zealots and the Herodians, not to mention the Judaism which John the Baptist practiced, which was similar to that of the Essenes. Most HRM teachers are advocating a return to modern Orthodox Judaism. But even within Orthodox Judaism, there are different types.

This keeping of a Talmudic form of the faith is not a rediscovering of the Jewish roots of the faith, but a return to apostate, synagogue Judaism. It is apostate because of their rejection of the Messiah. I am not saying there is nothing we can learn from these sources. Yet we must remember always that they were written by those who rejected the Messiah. We should be interpreting the Scriptures, not from rabbinic sources, but by the testimony of the Messiah Himself and His apostles.

Our True Hebrew Roots

There is a profound difference between the Judaism many HRM devotees practice and the true Hebrew roots of the faith found in Holy Scripture. The New Testament makes clear what the root is that sustains both Jewish and Gentile believers. In the eleventh chapter of Romans, Paul uses the metaphor of the olive tree to describe the relationship of Jewish and Gentile believers to the fathers, Abraham, Isaac, and Jacob (Romans 11:17-24). This teaching on the olive tree is part of a broader section that must first be understood if we are to grasp the significance of the olive tree metaphor (Romans 9-11).

It is possible that when Paul wrote Romans, Jews were returning to Rome after being banished by the edict of Claudius (Acts 18:2). The withdrawal of Jews from the church in Rome might have been understood by Gentiles as evidence that God was no longer saving Jews. Paul emphatically denies this, though, insisting that God is still saving Jews, albeit only a remnant (Romans 11:5). In fact, he begins this section by teaching that the true Israel was never the physical nation at all (as made clear by the rejection of Ishmael and Esau, who were also physical descendants) but the remnant of Jews who believed (Romans 9:6-13). In Paul's own words, "Not all who are descended from Israel belong to Israel" (Romans 9:6b).

To prove this (that the true Israel was the remnant), Paul quotes from an episode in the life of Elijah in which Elijah complains to God that he alone is righteous, having not bowed the knee to Baal (Romans 11:2-4). What does God say to him? He tells him that He has faithfully preserved a remnant who has not bowed the knee (Romans 11:5). Paul's conclusion? Just as the majority of Israelites in Elijah's day had become apostate except for a remnant chosen by God, so also the majority of Israelites in the present (Paul's day) had apostatized, having rejected Jesus'

Messiahship. But in the same way, God now had a remnant of Israelites who truly believed.

Before attempting to understand Paul's use of the metaphor of the olive tree in chapter 11, It is imperative that we first answer the question Paul begins chapter 11 with: "I ask, then, has God rejected his people?" (Romans 11:1):

> Now there are two possibilities concerning the meaning of Paul's question. First, he could be asking, "Did God reject Israel as a nation of people and their future salvation?" The second possibility is that he could be asking, "Did God utterly reject Israel so that no more Israelites will ever be saved?" Paul makes it clear that the meaning of his question is certainly the latter because his answer in verse 1 is that God is presently saving a remnant: "By no means (God has not rejected His people)! I am an Israelite myself, a descendant of Abraham, from the tribe of Benjamin." The evidence—that Paul is a Jew and that he has been saved—tells us that God has not utterly rejected Israel.[6]

Paul makes it clear throughout this section that God is still saving Israelites, though the majority of those who now believe are Gentiles. The best way to demonstrate that is through the metaphor of the olive tree. The olive was used throughout the Old Testament as a symbol for Israel (Jeremiah 11:16, Hosea 14:5-6). There are two primary reasons Israel was portrayed in Scripture as an olive tree. First, it is known for its *longevity* in that some olive trees have been known to last for centuries. In fact, some of the olives in the Garden of Gethsemane are believed to be almost two thousand years old.

But the second reason (and perhaps the most important) is they are known for their luxurious *fruit*. Even the smallest root left in the ground will continue to push new shoots upward into the sky in unwavering steadfast devotion to continuing to bear fruit throughout time. No wonder King David speaks of being "like a green olive tree in the house of God" (Psalm 52:8a). For this reason, the olive was the perfect metaphor for both the longevity and fruitfulness God had purposed for Israel:

> But if some of the branches were broken off, and you, although a wild olive shoot, were grafted in among the others and now share in the nourishing root of the olive tree, do not be arrogant toward the branches. If you are, remember it is not you who support the root, but the root that supports you. Then you will say, "Branches were broken off so that I might be grafted in." That is true. They were broken off because of their unbelief, but you stand fast through faith. So do not become proud, but fear. For if God did not spare the natural branches, neither will he spare you. Note then the kindness and the severity of God: severity toward those who have fallen, but God's kindness to you, provided you continue in his kindness. Otherwise you too will be cut off. And even they, if they do not continue in their unbelief, will be grafted in, for God has the power to graft them in again. For if you were cut from what is by nature a wild olive tree, and grafted, contrary to nature, into a cultivated olive tree, how much more will these, the natural branches, be grafted back into their own olive tree.
>
> — Romans 11:17-24

It seems clear that Paul is writing these words for the Gentiles in the Roman church who thought God was no longer saving Jews. Paul reminds them that it is much easier for God to graft the natural branches back into the original olive tree than to graft 'against nature' those whom he identifies as "wild olive shoots" (Romans 11:17). They (natural branches) were cut off because of unbelief, but through faith, they can be restored.

But we should pay special attention to what he says about the root system supporting both of them (Romans 11:18). Scholars and Bible commentators have debated for centuries what Paul means by the phrase the "root that supports you" in Romans 11:18. Like scholar N.T. Wright, some suggest it is the Messiah Himself. But I agree with Tim Holland, who writes, "Paul saw its root to represent the promises made to Abraham and its branches to represent his spiritual offspring—believing Jews and Gentiles who are justified and made holy by the same faith as their *father.*" [7]

I agree with the majority of scholars who see the Patriarchs (Abraham, Isaac, and Jacob) and specifically the promises made to Abraham as the root sustaining both Jewish and Gentile believers. And as Holland stated, the branches represent his spiritual offspring, believing Jews and Gentiles. In other words, it is Abraham and the promises made to him that is the root supporting all believers. This is our true root system. Jews are not connected to the tree because they share in Abraham's physicality (though they do), but because they share in the faith of Abraham. Abraham's seed was not a physical people, as Paul makes clear in Romans 9. Even though Abraham gave birth physically to Ishmael, he was rejected as an heir, God choosing Isaac in his place (Romans 9:8-9). Also, Abraham's son Isaac fathered Esau, but he also was rejected (Romans 9:10-13). What is Paul teaching? That Abraham's true descendants are those who are not merely physically descended from their father, but those he has chosen beforehand and who are justified by faith, just as their father Abraham was.

One thing is certain: *the root system that supports believers is not Moses and the Law.* Neither is it to be found in the Law and the traditions which have grown up around it. Those in the HRM who are advocating that Gentiles practice Rabbinic Judaism under the guise of being reconciled to their Hebrew roots are deceiving them. Gentile believers in Abraham's Seed (Galatians 3:16) are already reconciled to their Hebrew roots without having to practice Judaism.

Tradition or Scripture?

It cannot be stressed enough that the real issue is where we are deriving our authority from *tradition* or *Scripture.* Many in the HRM are seeking their identity in Talmudic Judaism and its outward practices. While believers are free to practice any tradition they choose, I believe that many in the HRM are not just practicing these things because of personal convictions they hold but because they want to live a Jewish lifestyle. In many cases, this includes keeping kosher (dietary laws) despite what Scripture teaches about the abrogation of these laws in the New Testament (Mark 7:14-19).

In His conflict with Jewish leaders of the day, Jesus condemned them for allowing their traditions to nullify the Word of God. The majority of HRM teachers would say they are keeping the Word of God, while most of the Church has forsaken God's commandments. But as we shall see in section four of this book, such a view can only be sustained by interpreting the New Testament in the light of the Old rather than the Old Testament in the light of the New.

In the next chapter, we will focus entirely on answering the question: Why are the majority of HRM devotees Gentiles?

What is the basis for this universal appeal to non-Jews? As we will see, there isn't one standard answer to this question. Yet, there is one reason that stands out more than others in providing an answer.

CHAPTER 12

Why the Attraction?

It is an indisputable fact that the majority of those participating in the HRM today are not Jews but Gentiles. This is true even in the makeup of most Messianic synagogues, which is surprising, considering that Messianic Judaism is touted as the primary way Jews would hear the Gospel. Stan Telchin, the author of the book *Messianic Judaism is Not Christianity*, also points out that the majority of those who attend messianic congregations are not Jews but Gentiles:

> I know that the overwhelming majority of Jewish believers do not attend Messianic synagogues. It has been suggested that less than five percent of the Jewish believers in the United States attend them. Many Jewish people who I have brought to such synagogues have told me they felt as though they were looking at a caricature—an imitation and not the real thing.[1]

Why are so many Gentiles attracted to messianic congregations and the HRM? What is the appeal for non-Jewish believers to leave their churches on a quest to discover their Jewish roots? There is more than one answer to this question, but the simplest one is the hidden (and sometimes not so hidden) desire to *be*

Jewish. Many Gentile believers, having concluded it is far better to be a Jewish believer than a Gentile believer, have embraced the HRM as a way of becoming Jewish—if not *physically*, at least religiously and culturally. Through HRM teaching instructing them to observe the Torah, many Gentiles are convinced they are now Jewish.

This, of course, is a fantasy; a person born a Jew can do nothing to change that. If they're born a Jew, they will die a Jew. The same is true of a man or woman born a Gentile; they can never become Jewish, even though they may practice Judaism. Of course, Gentiles can technically become Jews by undergoing a conversion process in Judaism. Still, that person undergoing the conversion process while outwardly practicing the Jewish faith still remains a Gentile when it comes to the flesh. Nothing can ever change that.

A Jewish Heart

Many Gentiles in the Messianic Jewish movement, as well as many in the HRM, speak of having received a "Jewish" heart. Stan Telchin explains the appeal for Gentiles to join messianic congregations:

> I can understand why Gentiles are attracted to
> Messianic congregations. They love the music. They
> want to learn about the Jewish roots of their faith.
> They enjoy learning about the Jewish holidays and
> even enjoy singing Hebrew songs. And certainly
> they enjoy the feeling of being a family.[2]

Once receiving a Jewish heart, many testify to having a love for all things Jewish (food, music, history, etc.). Is there a

Scriptural basis for this? Many of these believers see this love for all things Jewish as the means by which they (Gentiles) may provoke to jealousy unbelieving Jews, in the same way Paul hoped his ministry would do (Romans 11:13). This may account for why the majority of Jews today have come to the Lord through Gentile witness. It also may explain why many Gentile believers have such a deep love for the Jewish people. Due to the fact that the Jew was blinded so that Gentiles could come into the kingdom, they feel they now owe them a debt of gratitude (Romans 11:19). So it is not surprising that God has put a love in the hearts of many Gentile Christians for the Jewish people.

But in actuality, there is more at work here than an appreciation for what Gentiles now enjoy because of Jewish unbelief. As stated previously, many Gentile believers are persuaded that being a Jewish believer is far better than merely being a Gentile believer. Since they weren't born Jewish, the closest thing to being a Jew is by living a Jewish lifestyle. Rather than relishing in the fact that both Jew and Gentile are now one in the body of Messiah (Ephesians 2:14-15), they now seek their identity in the flesh.

To be sure, there are benefits to being born Jewish, as Paul reminds the Roman church (Romans 3:1-2). The Gospel naturally came to the Jew first because of the promises made to them (Romans 1:17). Yet because of what God did in redeeming us through Messiah, the two (Jew and Gentile) are now united in one body through his death on the cross (Ephesians 2:16). That does not mean that the distinction between Jew and Gentile does not still exist; it does, in the same way, the distinction between the genders still exists, even though Paul states there is no longer male or female (Galatians 3:28). When it comes to our standing before God, though, all such distinctions are nullified. God doesn't love me more or treat me better because I am a Jewish believer than he does a Gentile believer. All have the same standing before God, having access to God through the blood of Jesus (Hebrews 10:19). The only thing that matters is that we are both one in Messiah:

> As a Jew who loves being Jewish, I found this both fascinating and disturbing. What I was reading seemed to be saying that my Jewishness did not matter to God, and that other believers Gentileness did not matter to God. In God's sight we were equally New creations. I remember scratching my head and repeating: No matter whether we are Jews or Gentiles; no matter our race, color or nationality; no matter our education; no matter our social standing or our occupation—if Jesus Is Lord of our lives, we are joined together spiritually as new creations.[3]

Harmless Cultural Preference or Another Gospel?

Many in the HRM claim that they are simply promoting harmless cultural preferences every believer is free to embrace. Is that true? Is the HRM encouraging people to practice mere Jewish cultural preferences? Or is it teaching another Gospel?

I am convinced that what many Gentiles are being taught by many HRM teachers today goes way beyond mere cultural preferences and, in some cases, amounts to the preaching of another Gospel. As previously stated, Paul doesn't commend the Galatians in his letter for their embrace of harmless cultural preferences but accuses them of a wholesale departure from the Gospel (Galatians 1:6). It would be one thing if HRM teachers merely used the Law for the sake of Jewish evangelism as Paul himself did. But in this case, Gentiles are being taught that they must be Torah-observant if they want to live righteous lives. What a far cry this was from the apostle who said,

> But whatever gain I had, I counted as loss for the sake of Christ. Indeed, I count everything as loss because of the surpassing worth of knowing Christ Jesus, my Lord. For his sake I have suffered the loss of all things and count them as rubbish, in order that I may gain Christ and be found in him, not having a righteousness of my own that comes from the law, but that which comes through faith in Christ, the righteousness from God that depends on faith.
>
> — Philippians 3:7-9

Is that what most of those in the HRM are taking away from what they are being taught—that men and women must find a righteousness *apart* from the law? Far from it. Instead, many are hearing that in order to be reconciled to their Jewish roots, they must become Torah observant. HRM teachers may couch it as nothing more than becoming *culturally* Jewish, but looking carefully at what they are teaching, it is apparent that few share the same view the apostle Paul expressed in Philippians 3 when it comes to terms with their personal identity in Christ.

Gentiles Are Not Second-Hand Citizens

One of the reasons many Gentiles are drawn to the HRM is that they have been made to feel like second-class citizens by their Jewish counterparts. Since (according to many HRM teachers) it is much better to be a Jewish believer than a non-Jewish one, it is not difficult to understand why Gentiles are eager to come under this teaching. As previously stated, it allows them, at least in practice, to be Jewish.

Some assume that Paul is teaching the superiority of Jews over Gentiles when referring to Jews as "natural" branches and Gentiles as "wild olive shoots" (Romans 11:17). But nothing could be further from the truth. What he means when referring to Israelites as the "natural" branches is that they were the first ones chosen to be branches in the olive tree. But that doesn't mean they are of greater value than the wild olive branches. If it did, it would be inconsistent with what Paul said earlier in the Roman letter; that Jews and Gentiles are both "under sin" (Romans 3:9). In other words, both are on a level playing field when it comes to condemnation and justification.

If anything, the New Testament actually teaches that there was a shift from Jewish superiority to Gentile primacy. This can be seen in various portions of Scripture, none perhaps more clearly than the parable of the Vineyard Owner found in Matthew 21:33-44:

> "Hear another parable. There was a master of a house who planted a vineyard and put a fence around it and dug a winepress in it and built a tower and leased it to tenants, and went into another country. When the season for fruit drew near, he sent his servants to the tenants to get his fruit. And the tenants took his servants and beat one, killed another, and stoned another. Again he sent other servants, more than the first. And they did the same to them. Finally, he sent his son to them, saying, 'They will respect my son.' But when the tenants saw the son, they said to themselves, 'This is the heir.

Come, let us kill him and have his inheritance.' And
they took him and threw him out of the vineyard
and killed him. When therefore the owner of the
vineyard comes, what will he do to those tenants?"
They said to him, "He will put those wretches
to a miserable death and let out the vineyard to
other tenants who will give him the fruits in their
seasons."

— Matthew 21:33-44

It seems clear from the parable that the master of the house
who planted a vineyard and did everything he could to protect
it represents God. The tenants he leased it to were the Israelites,
who were called to tend the vineyard so that the master could
receive the fruit. The servants whom he sent that were beaten and
stoned were the prophets. When they didn't receive his servants,
he sent his son, whom they promptly killed. Jesus then asked
the Jewish leaders the question, "Therefore, when the owner of
the vineyard comes, what will he do to those farmers?" Notice
how they answered: "He will completely destroy those terrible
men, and lease his vineyard to other farmers who will give him
his fruit at the harvest" (Matthew 21:41). This is undoubtedly
a reference to the judgment of God, which fell on Israel when
both city and temple were destroyed in AD 70. Though the New
Covenant had been firmly in place for almost forty years, it was
not until the temple was removed that the last vestiges of the
Old Covenant were completely removed. What does Jesus say
the result will be? "Therefore I tell you, the kingdom of God will
be taken away from you and given to a people producing its fruit"
(Matthew 21:43).

Who are the people and the nation that the kingdom has
now been given to? There is little doubt Jesus is referring to the

Church comprised largely of Gentiles. They are the "new nation" which produces the fruit of the kingdom. As Paul's olive tree metaphor describes in Romans 11, God is still saving a remnant of Jews throughout the Church Age, yet the majority of believers are now Gentiles. Historically, it was only as the majority of Jews were hardened that Gentiles began to be brought in.

Although He was sent primarily to the lost sheep of the house of Israel during His earthly ministry, there were times Jesus ministered to Gentiles as an early foreshadowing of the truth that Gentiles would one day be united together with believing Israelites through the Messiah's death. The Syrophoenician woman is a prime example of that (Mark 7:24-30). Fresh off His debate with Jewish leaders about true defilement (Mark 7:1-23), Jesus deliberately went into the Gentile region of Tyre and Sidon (the first time He had actually wandered beyond the borders of the land of Israel). His going there was deliberate, a fitting preview of the eventual proclamation of the Gospel to the Gentile world. A Gentile woman came to Him, pleading that He "cast the demon out of her daughter" (Mark 7:26b). Jesus reminds her that it is not appropriate to "take the children's bread and give it to the dogs" (Mark 7:27b). The woman agrees but responds with a parable of her own; that "even the dogs under the table eat the children's crumbs" (Mark 7:28b). Consequently, Jesus heals her daughter.

Other examples abound of Jesus' ministry to Gentiles during His earthly ministry, such as His healing of the Roman centurion's servant (Luke 7:1-10). While they may be random acts, He made it clear that Gentiles, as well as Jews, were being invited into the messianic kingdom. His parable of the Wedding Feast for the Son is perhaps the clearest evidence of this (Matthew 22:1-14). When Israelites, who were the first to be invited to the feast, refused to come (Matthew 22:8), the king orders his servants to "go therefore to the main roads and invite to the wedding feast as many as you find. And those servants went out into the roads and gathered all whom they found, both bad and good" (Matthew 22:9-10a). This clearly sets forth that eventually, Gentiles would be invited to the feast.

These events undergird that Gentiles were now being called, not as second-class citizens behind their Jewish counterparts, but as those who would eventually be given full fellowship with Israel in the Messiah. It was not until Paul arrived on the scene that the full measure of understanding of the acceptance of the Gentiles was fully realized. Paul speaks in the Ephesian letter of his personal insight into this mystery, that "the Gentiles are fellow heirs, members of the same body, and partakers of the promise in Christ Jesus through the gospel" (Ephesians 3:6). Paul's language is clear: Gentiles are not second-class citizens but full partners with their Jewish counterparts in the Gospel.

Summing It Up

Many Gentiles involved in the HRM have gone beyond merely wanting to discover the Jewish roots of their faith to wanting to be Jewish themselves. Though not Jewish in the flesh, they have now found a way to do so by receiving a "Jewish heart."

But we have no evidence in the New Testament that Gentile believers were taught to get a Jewish heart and become Torah observant. They were certainly taught through the apostle Paul's example to love and pray for Israel (Romans 9:1-3, Romans 10:1) as well as to remember that their own standing with God was based on the natural branches of unbelief (Romans 11:11). But nowhere do we find Paul or any of the other apostles teaching non-Jewish believers that they must keep the Sabbath, the dietary laws, and the Jewish feasts. There is no need for Gentiles to do these things since being outwardly Jewish now has nothing to do with being members of the people of God.

The truth is, Gentiles who believe are already *one* with their Jewish counterparts in the Gospel. God has forged from both "one new man." While Gentiles still have an obligation to pray for that remnant of Israel, which God has called to Himself, that is a far cry from teaching they must now adopt a thoroughly Jewish lifestyle.

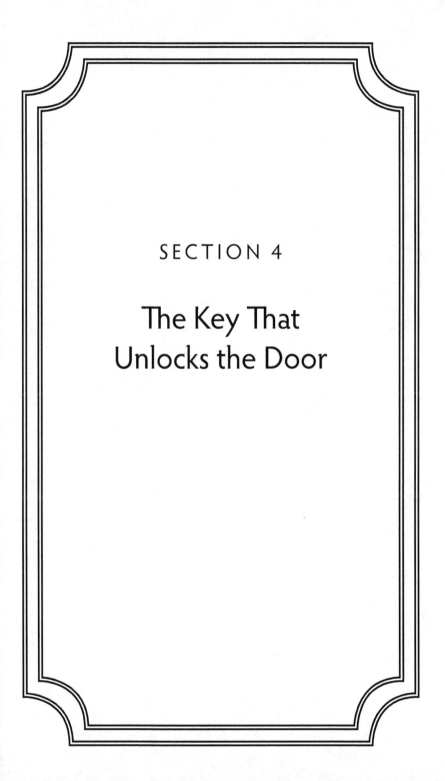

SECTION 4

The Key That Unlocks the Door

CHAPTER 13

A Mistaken Hermeneutic

In this section of this book, we take a look at those principles by which HRM teachers interpret Scripture. The word commonly used for the study of the principles of interpretation is *hermeneutics*. Don't be intimidated by that word; it's a fancy term for the "theory and methodology of interpreting biblical texts." Simply stated, it is the methods we use to interpret the Bible. Whether we are familiar with that big word or not, everyone who reads the Bible practices hermeneutics in that they attempt to interpret what they are reading. Even though they may not have given any thought to the methods they use (most haven't), they try and understand what they are reading.

The great need, therefore, is to make sure we are using the right methods when attempting to interpret the Scriptures. There are proper methods, and there are improper methods. With a little bit of training, anyone can master basic hermeneutical methods so as to understand Scripture.

The focus of this chapter is to expose the faulty hermeneutic used by many HRM teachers when it comes to interpreting the Old Testament. What is that improper method? *It is interpreting the New Testament in the light of the Old rather than interpreting the Old in the light of the New.* In other words, they are not viewing the Hebrew Bible through the lens of how Jesus and the apostles viewed them. This is critical when it comes to understanding much of the teaching in the HRM today.

To be fair, it goes both ways. We must learn not only to interpret the Old in the light of the New but the New in the light of the Old as well. But if we want to gain a proper New Testament understanding of the Old Testament, we must learn to interpret it through the lens of how Jesus and the apostles did. They provide us with a proper hermeneutic for interpreting the Law and the Prophets. In the next chapter, we will focus on seeing that proper hermeneutic at work in the wonderful letter to the Hebrews.

Hermeneutical Framework for Hebrew Roots Movement

To understand the hermeneutic most HRM teachers use, let's first look at the following description at the website ChurchWord. org:

> The Hebrew Roots movement has a hermeneutic framework which begins with the Torah and works its way out from there. This is to say that Scripture is interpreted in light of the Torah. On the other hand, the majority of Protestants hold that the Scriptures are to be interpreted in light of newer, clearer revelation and that the Old Testament saints were seeing a cloudy shadow of the things which were to be revealed later in the New Testament. This Protestant hermeneutic principle is called the analogy of faith.[1]

The HRM adopts the Torah as the standard by which they view the entire Old Testament. The writer of this article goes on to say,

> I would like to submit, in this post, that the key issue which causes a movement such as the Hebrew Roots has to do with a faulty hermeneutic. In Deconstructing Islam I argue that it is important that a source which is seen to be special revelation from God ought to also come with its own standard of interpretation. Without this, I argue, that a theistic position which does not come with its own standard of interpretation is indefensible and therefore false. I think that the hermeneutic utilized within the Hebrew Roots movement is just that, an indefensible, man-made, standard of interpretation.[2]

The writer points out in this article the faulty hermeneutic by which HRM teachers interpret the Scriptures. Here is how he describes it:

> Basically, what the Hebraist does is read the Torah and say to himself, "this is the word of God so it must be perfect, so it therefore must also never go away." I can respect their reverence for God's Word and desire to see it as something which is always true and never fading (I agree). However, in order to see God's Word as always true, there is no need to believe that the Old Covenant economy eclipses the New Covenant economy. In fact, this causes one to lose sight of the entire point of the Scriptures. For instance, Christians see the Old Testament as

always true because the revelation within reveals to us, further and further, God's overall redemptive plan. It is always going to be true that Christ is foreshadowed in Genesis, (Genesis 3:15) it will always be true that God's Law served a purpose for the historical nation of Israel, it will always be true that Old Testament prophecy served to reveal the future coming of the Messiah. However, to think those who believe God's Word must always be true must also carry over the entire Law of the Old Testament is fallacious. What else must we also carry over in order to be consistent with this logic? Judges? Prophets?[3]

We can appreciate the movement's devotion to the Torah. They want to see it as "perfect, so it, therefore, must also never go away." But in doing so, they are committed to the conviction that the "Old Covenant economy eclipses the New Covenant economy." The end result (according to the writer of this article) is that people "lose sight of the entire point of the Scriptures." While the Torah serves as the historical and religious foundation for the entire Old Testament, it cannot be separated from the rest of the Hebrew Bible.

To understand this properly, we must have a basic understanding of the threefold division of the Hebrew canon of Scripture. This is important because Hebraists (and most HRM teachers) consider the Torah to be more inspired than any other division of the Hebrew Bible:

Jewish tradition considers the three divisions of Scripture to be sacred and inspired by God but distinguishes between degrees of inspiration. The

> Torah is more inspired than the Prophetic books,
> as it is a more direct communication from God to
> Moses. Then the books of the Prophets are more
> inspired than the Writings because the Writings
> result from the less intense form of communication
> known as the "Holy Spirit." To emphasize these
> differences, pious Jews will never place a book of
> lesser inspiration on top of one that is considered
> more inspired.[4]

In a previous chapter, we talked about how the Church has divided the Old Testament into a fourfold division: Torah (first five books), Historical (Joshua, Judges, Ruth, 1 Samuel, 2 Samuel, 1 Kings, 2 Kings, 1 Chronicles, 2 Chronicles), Prophetical (Isaiah, Jeremiah, Ezekiel, Daniel, Minor Prophets) and Poetical (Job, Psalms, Proverbs, Ecclesiastes, Song of Songs). But most in the HRM place the Torah in the highest place when it comes to authority. While I would agree that the Torah is first when it comes to a historical foundation for the rest of the Bible, there is nothing in the Bible itself that tells us that we should view it as containing a higher level of inspiration.

Messiah Validates the Three Divisions of the Hebrew Bible

Earlier, we alluded to Luke's account of Jesus' appearance to the apostles in the Upper Room (Luke 24:13-49). In these accounts, Jesus validates the threefold division of the Hebrew Bible. Actually, there are two accounts that are blended together in the final chapter of his Gospel. The two share one common theme; that Jesus is the interpretive key to understanding the Hebrew Bible (Old Testament). Let's look briefly at both accounts.

The first account recorded in Luke is the appearance of the resurrected Messiah to two disciples on the road to Emmaus (Luke 24:13-16). Unaware at first that it was Jesus who had joined them, He asked them what they had been talking about while on the road. They began to relate to this Stranger the mighty words and deeds done by the Lord during those days. They also conveyed their disappointment that He was not the one who "redeemed Israel" (Luke 24:21). Besides, some women were at the tomb early that morning and reported seeing a vision of angels who said He was alive (Luke 24:22-23). This was confirmed by some of the apostles who went to the tomb and did not find His body (Luke 24:24).

Still unaware who was speaking to them, He rebuked them for their unbelief: "O foolish ones, and slow of heart to believe all that the prophets have spoken! Was it not necessary that the Christ should suffer these things and enter into his glory?" (Luke 24:25-26). This was followed by an in-depth Bible study in which "beginning with Moses and all the Prophets, he interpreted to them in all the Scriptures the things concerning himself" (Luke 24:27). The Greek word translated as "interpreted" is "diermeneuo" and means to explain, interpret, or translate. This word is derived from the root word "meneuo," the root from which the word hermeneutics is derived. They would later speak of how their hearts "burned within them while he talked with them on the road and opened the Scriptures" (Luke 24:32).

The second account is found at the end of chapter twenty-four. They (the two on the road to Emmaus) immediately went to Jerusalem to tell the apostles they had seen the Lord. When they arrived, they discovered He had already appeared to Simon (Luke 24:34). While gathered behind closed doors, Jesus Himself came and stood in their midst (Luke 24:36). Luke records that at that time, He "opened their minds to understand the Scriptures" (Luke 24:44). As previously stated, since these men were Jews and grew up reading and memorizing the Hebrew Bible, he was not introducing them to the Hebrew Bible for the first time. What Luke means is that He took them through each of the three divisions of the Hebrew Bible (Law, Prophets, Psalms), demonstrating how they were now to be interpreted in the light of His Coming.

As we saw earlier, that certainly includes his fulfilling of certain predictions made about Him in the Old Testament, such as being born of a virgin in the town of Bethlehem. But as previously pointed out, it also means not only that he fulfilled certain predictions but "filled full" its history so as to give it new meaning. Take, for example, Luke's account of the Transfiguration (Luke 9:28-36). After bringing Peter, John, and James up a mountain, Jesus was praying when "the appearance of his face was altered, and his clothing became dazzling white" (Luke 9:29). Suddenly, two men appeared, Moses and Elijah, who were talking with him (Luke 9:30). But take special notice of what Luke says the subject of their conversation was: "And behold, two men were talking with him, Moses and Elijah, who appeared in glory and spoke of his *departure*, which he was about to accomplish at Jerusalem" (Luke 9:30-31; italics mine).

It is only as we discover that the Greek word for *departure* in this text is *exodos* that the story suddenly takes on new meaning. It is, of course, the technical word for Israel's departure from Egypt as told in the book by the same name (Exodus). What is Luke saying by using that word in reference to his soon coming departure from this world? It is that this is the *true* Exodus—not the departure of Israel from political bondage but the departure of the Jewish Messiah from this world in death. As Israel left their captivity due to the plagues visited upon Egypt, so also the Son of God was visited upon by the judgment of God so that God's people may go free.

An Apostolic Hermeneutic

Jesus made it clear in the Upper Room that the Old Testament was now to be interpreted in the light of the New Covenant inaugurated by His coming. He gave to them what might be called an *apostolic* hermeneutic—the method of interpreting Scripture used by Jesus and the apostles. For the apostles in the New Testament, every story, prophecy, event, and instruction was now to be interpreted in the light of His first coming. As Peter said in his sermon in Acts, "All the prophets who have spoken, from Samuel and those who came after him, also proclaimed *these* days" (Acts 3:24; italics mine). Jesus summed it up well in John's Gospel when he said, "You search the Scriptures because you think that in them you have eternal life; and it is they that bear witness about me, yet you refuse to come to me that you may have life" (John 5:39). The whole of Scripture bears witness to him. Sadly, instead of coming to Him to receive life, they engaged in an endless search of the Scriptures, thinking this to be the pathway to life.

Turning from the Gospels to the New Testament letters, we find the apostolic hermeneutic further defined. Paul's entire understanding of the doctrine of justification by faith alone is based on a statement Moses made regarding Abraham recorded in Genesis 15:6. After God had told him to "look toward heaven and number the stars, if you are able to number them" (Genesis 15:5a), God spoke to him, "So shall your offspring be." Moses reports Abraham's response: "And He believed the LORD, and he counted it to him as righteousness" (Genesis 15:6).

So the apostle concludes, "It is those of faith who are the sons of Abraham" (Galatians 3:7). The true sons of Abraham are not physical descendants but those who have the faith of Abraham. For "the Scripture, foreseeing that God would justify the Gentiles by faith, preached the Gospel beforehand to Abraham, saying, "In you shall all the nations be blessed" (Galatians 3:8b).

Paul teaches that the true children of God were never those who were mere physical descendants, but those who were children by faith as made clear in his statement, "not all are children of Abraham because they are his offspring, but 'Through Isaac shall your offspring be named.'" (Romans 9:7). Even though Ishmael was Abraham's first son, he was rejected as an heir, God choosing Isaac in his place (Romans 9:8-9). And Rebekah, Isaac's wife, when she had conceived twins in her womb before the children were even born, "in order that God's purpose of election might continue, not because of works but because of him who calls— she was told, "The older will serve the younger" (Romans 9:11-12).

Notice how in both Romans and Galatians, Paul interprets the Old Testament in the light of the New. *The New Testament revelation of Jesus is the interpretive key to understanding the Old Testament*. The same is true in the letters that Peter wrote. In writings to believers, Peter pulls from various places throughout the Hebrew Bible, using language which had previously been reserved only for Israel:

> But you are a chosen race, a royal priesthood, a holy nation, a people for his own possession, that you may proclaim the excellencies of him who called you out of darkness into his marvelous light. Once you were not a people, but now you are God's people; once you had not received mercy, but now you have received mercy.
>
> — 1 Peter 2:9-10

"Chosen race" is language summarizing Deuteronomy 10:15: "Yet the Lord set his heart in love on your fathers and chose their offspring after them, you above all peoples, as you are this day." This is conveyed in the opening greetings of Peter's first epistle by the word "eklektos," translated by the English word "elect." The Church is now the *true* chosen people, God calling both Jews and Gentiles to be a people for His name. "A royal priesthood" refers to the fact that God has called all of His people to be "a kingdom, priests to his God and Father, to him be glory and dominion forever and ever. Amen" (Revelation 1:6). "Holy nation" also summarizes Deuteronomy 7:6. The phrase "a people for his own possession" comes right from the words God spoke at Sinai to His covenant people gathered at the mount after leaving Egypt. "Treasured possession" is the translation of the Hebrew term "segullah," which is most likely a quote from Isaiah 43:21, since the verse goes on to refer to God's chosen people as proclaiming the "excellencies of him who called you out of darkness into his marvelous light" (1 Peter 2:9). He closes this statement with a clear reference to Hosea 1:9-10 where God spoke to Hosea to name His son "not my people"; a prophetic announcement that those who were physically Jews were now rejected as His people and those who were formerly not His people (Gentiles) were now "children of the living God" (Hosea 1:10).

The letter to the Hebrews is a marvelous record of what the messianic hermeneutic consists of. It is so important, I have devoted the entire following chapter to it. It is vital that we grasp how the writer of Hebrews views what has come in Jesus as God's final word to the human race. The Revelation also demonstrates the way the apostles interpreted the Hebrew Bible. It depends entirely on the Old Testament for its understanding, as Eric Lyons makes clear:

Of the 404 verses in the book of Revelation, seemingly 278 of them make some allusion to the Old Testament. That is 68.8% of the verses! And some of these verses contain two, or even three, allusions to the Old Testament. The book of Revelation does not tell whence these allusions came. However, by a careful study of the Bible, we can understand that most of them come from the prophetic books of Isaiah, Ezekiel, Daniel, and Zechariah. Thus, it would be good to have some knowledge of the Old Testament before studying the book of Revelation. For example, before reading the apostle John's vision of the seven golden lampstands in Revelation 1, a student should realize that such language had been used when Zechariah had a similar vision in chapter 4 of the book that bears his name. Prior to reading John's vision of a "new heaven" and "new earth" (Revelation 21:1), a person might want to read Isaiah 65 and 66 to understand that such language had been used long before Revelation ever was written.[5]

Since we don't know our Old Testament, it is not surprising that we really don't understand the Revelation. As long as we turn to the *USA Today* to see if it has been fulfilled rather than to Moses and the Prophets, we will remain strangers to its essential message.

Looking Ahead

To prepare for the next chapter, I suggest the reader do a walk through the New Testament book of Hebrews. This book is the sourcebook of apostolic interpretation of the Hebrew Bible. In the next chapter, we focus entirely on how the writer of Hebrews interprets the Old Testament.

I have often been asked if people in the HRM even read the book of Hebrews. It's actually a good question. It seems if they did, they would not be able to hold many of the views they espouse. That's because Hebrews challenge Jews who believe in Jesus to leave behind the shadows of Old Testament religion and embrace the substance which has come in the Messiah. I explore this more fully in the next chapter.

CHAPTER 14

The Letter to the Hebrews and the HRM

It should not be surprising that Hebrews is one of my favorite books in Scripture. As a Jew who believes Jesus is the Messiah, it not only provides me with a rationale for faith in Jesus as the Messiah it also teaches me what it means to be a member of God's chosen people. Each time I read this majestic letter, I gain a new appreciation of the arguments he (or she) makes from the Old Testament.

More than any other book in Scripture, Hebrews attempts to make sense out of fifteen hundred years of Old Testament history, promises, covenants, and rituals. And it does so to set forth the powerful truth that what has come in the Messiah is so much *better* than everything that preceded it! The Messiah has come and introduced a brand new order, superior in every way to what existed under the old order.

One of the ways the writer of Hebrews communicates this is by referring to everything in the Old Covenant as a "*shadow of the good things to come* instead of the true form of these realities" (Hebrews 10:1; italics mine). By referring to them as shadows, the author doesn't mean they weren't real; they were, in fact, real personages, real events, and real rituals. But they were not complete in themselves, being mere reflections of reality. The fullness of those things would not be known until the Messiah came. Then, those shadows would give place to the substance which has come in Jesus.

I once heard a Bible teacher refer to Israel's life under the Old Covenant as the doll stage of religion. When women are little girls, they play with dolls. Why do little girls play with dolls? Undoubtedly, it is unconscious preparation for the day when they'll trade in their dolls for the living baby. Under the Old Covenant era, Israel was given dolls to play with (the Law) until the time when God would ask them to trade in their dolls for the living baby. But we all know what happened. When the time came for them to trade in the dolls for the living baby, they killed him so they could go on playing with their dolls. And Israel continues to play with their dolls to this present day.

The Theme of Hebrews

What we know from the letter itself is that it was written to Jews who had come to faith in Jesus as the Messiah some time before the temple was destroyed in AD 70. We have no idea how they became believers or who preached to them since we know nothing about the author. Luke tells us in Acts that "a great many of the priests became obedient to the faith" (Acts 6:7b). Since there is such an emphasis on the priesthood of Messiah in this letter, it is possible the author was one of those priests who came to faith. Since God has not revealed it, it is purely conjecture.

What we do know is that these believers suffered greatly after coming to faith, some—going to prison, while others—losing all their possessions (Hebrews 10:34). It was very costly at that time to be a Jew and believe in Jesus (it can still be today). And that is the reason the author writes the letter; to encourage these believers not to throw away their confidence which has great reward (Hebrews 10:35). In the strongest language possible, the writer urges them not to succumb to the temptation to go back to the "shadow religion" of Judaism under the Old Covenant. In other words, the writer wants them to leave the Jewish shadows of the Old Testament so as to embrace all of the realities of the New Covenant.

How the writer seeks to do this sets forth the beauty and majesty of this book. He understands that as Jews, they were reticent to turn their back on fifteen hundred years of Hebrew history. Why should they since their religion was superior to anything in any other religion up to that time? What could be better than the Prophets or Moses or Aaron or the Temple? So the writer, knowing the difficulty they will have, turning their back on these things (especially in light of the fact that there was tremendous pressure on them to remain within the Jewish religion), goes back over each aspect of their history. His goal is to convince them that the things set forth in the Old Testament were not designed to be permanent but temporary. They served as shadows of the realities that would come under the New Covenant (Hebrews 10:1).

To grasp how the writer does that, let's look at the first paragraph of this majestic letter where the writer contrasts the prophets, God's spokesmen in the Old Testament, to the revelation the Son has brought (Hebrews 1:1-3). This paragraph, if properly understood, lays a foundation for how the writer treats the remainder of the letter. God spoke to Israel through these prophets at many different *times* during their history and in many different *ways*. In this paragraph, the writer contrasts that with God's final word, which He spoke in the last days in His Son: "Old Testament prophetic revelation has now received its end-times climax through God's Son. However highly the readership regarded that former revelation, the writer implied they must now listen most closely to the Son."[1]

The word of the Son is final because of His inherent superior nature, making the revelation He brings superior to all who preceded Him. He is the One who the Father has appointed to "inherit all things" and through whom He "formed the ages" (Hebrews 1:2). He goes on to describe him as the "radiance of the glory of God" (Hebrews 1:3). The word "radiance" is a Greek term rendered "brightness" in the KJV. Some versions use the word *effulgence*, an old word sometimes rendered by the term "out-raying." It specifically refers to the sun and its rays. The sun is too bright to look at directly; we only know the sun by means of its rays. That's exactly what the writer is saying by using this term. What the rays of the sun are to the sun, so the Son of God is to the Father. This is the writer's way of saying that it is only through Jesus that we truly can know the Father.

The writer follows it by saying the Messiah is "the exact *imprint* of his nature" (Hebrews 1:3; italics mine). The word imprint is the translation of the Greek word "charakter," a term used of the stamping of images on coins. Once a stamp is applied to the metal, the copy is an exact replica of the original. In the same way, Jesus is imprinted with the Father's nature so that He is the exact replica of the Father. Jesus Himself alluded to this when He told the Twelve in the upper room, "whoever has seen me has seen the Father?" (John 14:9). In other words, *Jesus is the perfect copy of the nature of the Father.* That is why when asked by Philip to reveal the Father, He said to him, "Have I been so long with you, and yet you have not come to know Me, Philip?" (John 14:9). To have seen the Son is to see the Father, for He is His exact representation.

This is followed by the writer's declaration that the Son now "upholds all things by the word of his power" (Hebrews 1:3). If there was ever a statement in the New Testament in which the deity of the Son is clearly taught, it is this. His word is so powerful through it; He sustains all He has created. The universe is not governed by impersonal force but by the power of the word of Jesus. That is the meaning of the statement which follows that "when He had made purification of sins, He sat down at the right hand of the Majesty on high" (Hebrews 1:3). The writer now anticipates the main focus of the later portions of the letter, which deals with the high priestly work of the Lord Jesus. He who now occupies the highest place in the universe from which He governs the world in the interests of the Church is the same One who took on human flesh and suffered so as to make purification for sin.

The remainder of the letter goes on to compare the Messiah to the angels through whose mediation the law was given; to Moses, who though being a great prophet was still a servant in the house while Jesus was a Son; to the Sabbath, which, while under the Old Covenant was a physical day of rest, is now a spiritual dimension we are bidden to inhabit; to Aaron, the high priest who, once a year, entered the Holy of holies with sprinkled blood for both himself and the people, but who is now a greater High Priest after a different order; to the Holy of holies, which, under the Old Covenant was a partition of the tabernacle and temple only the high priest could enter; a representation of the true tabernacle in heaven where the Messiah now permanently resides.

These things in the Old Testament were indeed good, but what the Messiah has introduced is so much *better*. No wonder that's the operative word of the epistle. The Messiah brings better *promises*, a better *covenant*, a better *sacrifice*, and a better *possession* (Hebrews 7:19, 7:22, 8:6, 9:23). They are better in the same way that a real person is better than his or her shadow.

Hebrews and the HRM

If it is true that Messiah has brought better things than what the Old Covenant offered, why do many in the HRM remain focused on the shadows rather than the substance? Why don't HRM teachers view the Old Testament the way the writer of Hebrews does? The simple answer is, they can't since Hebrews undermines many of the HRM's major tenets. So they either ignore it completely or, in some extreme cases, discredit it entirely.

Take, for example, what HRM teacher Monte Judah says about the letter to the Hebrews. He suggests Hebrews doesn't even belong in the Bible since it differs from the rest of Scripture. According to Judah, there are several contradictions in the book of Hebrews, which leads him to this conclusion:

> More specifically, the description of important
> historical events seem to be retold differently
> and quotations from the previous writings are
> misquoted leading to specific theological concepts
> that are very different. Within the paradigm,
> most Christians believe that everything written
> in Hebrews, particularly about the Law, is fully
> accurate and correct. They accept the conclusions
> and pronouncements of the writer about the
> Messiah based on the writer's representations of
> the Law, despite these misrepresentations. Because
> most Christians agree with the ultimate conclusions
> that the writer makes about Yeshua as the Messiah,
> they tend to overlook the differences and the faulty
> premises. Therefore the door is open for both those
> in the faith to advance an errant teaching and, worse
> yet, for those outside the faith to discredit Yeshua
> and our brethren in the faith using the paradigm

of the letter to the Hebrews as the basis for their challenge.[2]

He also questions the validity of the letter by casting doubts on whether it was written by a Hebrew since the writing is more Greek than Hebrew:

> The book is really an epistle entitled to the Hebrews, but as you will soon see, the writing and logic are Greek. It was written in Greek, quoting from Greek copies of the Scriptures, and using Greek definitions to explain and teach Hebraic things. The first paradigm about the book of Hebrews that needs to be explored is its Greek influence in thought. The paradigm most have of Hebrews is that it was written by a Hebrew (probably the Apostle Paul) to other Hebrews. So it is natural to think that it is solidly Hebrew in thought, because it quotes extensively from the 'Old Testament.' However, as you are about to discover, the definitions and teachings lifted from the Old Testament are Greek in thought.[3]

There is no hidden agenda when it comes to Monte Judah's intention since he states it clearly: "The book of Hebrews should be eliminated from the Bible!" Since he deems it to be nothing more than a "Greek" letter, he feels totally justified in dismissing it. But he forgets (or else doesn't know) that the most popular version of the Hebrew Bible in the first century and the one quoted frequently by Jesus and the apostles is the Septuagint, the Greek version of the Hebrew Bible translated into Greek around 150 BC. It literally means "translation of the seventy" because it was supposedly translated by seventy-two scholars. "Philo of Alexandria, who relied extensively on the Septuagint, says that the number of scholars was chosen by selecting six scholars from each of the twelve tribes of Israel."[4]

Some HRM teachers, such as Monte Judah, reject the Septuagint as being unreliable. Nevertheless, Pre-Christian Jews Philo and Josephus considered the Septuagint on equal standing with the Hebrew text. Manuscripts of the Septuagint have been found among the Qumran Scrolls at the Dead Sea and were thought to have been in use among Jews at the time. [5]

If they considered the Septuagint to be on equal standing with the Hebrew text, why don't HRM teachers like Monte Judah think so?

The obvious truth is, Judah rejects Hebrews not because it was written in Greek but due to its content. It sets forth the apostolic truth that everything Israel enjoyed in the Old Testament, such as angels, Moses, the land of Israel, the priesthood, the covenant, the temple, and the sacrifices, are now given new meaning in the Person and work of the Messiah, the Son of God. And that is exactly what many HRM teachers reject. Rather than viewing the Hebrew Bible as being fulfilled by Jesus, they view His coming as a means of establishing the Law.

Errors in Hebrews?

By far, the most direct way Monte Judah discredits the book of Hebrews is by suggesting there are errors in the letter. His most obvious one is Hebrews 9:3-4, where the writer states that

> Behind the second curtain was a second section
> called the Most Holy Place, having the golden altar
> of incense and the ark of the covenant covered on all
> sides with gold, in which was a golden urn holding

the manna, and Aaron's staff that budded, and the tablets of the covenant.

—Hebrews 9:3-4

Here is what Monte Judah says about this passage:

> There is a problem with this passage: And behind the second veil, there was a tabernacle which is called the Holy of Holies, having a golden altar of incense... (Hebrews 9:3-4). This part is not correct as written. The altar of incense is in the first sanctuary with the lampstand and table, not in the Holy of Holies with the Ark of the Covenant.[6]

How can Hebrews be trusted since (according to Judah) it so grossly errs in such a fundamental way as to place the altar of incense in the Holy of Holies? But there is a simple reason the writer of Hebrews places the altar of incense in the Holy of holies rather than the Holy place:

> While it is true that the "golden altar of incense" is outside the veil, the context here is that of the Day of Atonement (as we see in Heb 8 where the High Priest is in the Holy of Holies). On the day of atonement the High Priest would take incense from the golden altar of incense and place it in the Holy of Holies (Leviticus 16:12-13) so that Hebrews, in telling us that the Holy of Holies "had" the golden altar of incense is correct because it was being filled with incense from the altar.[7]

Let's look at another supposed error that Monte Judah asserts is found in Hebrews. He claims that the author changes the meaning from the Hebrew idea of covenant to the Greek concept of "will and testament" in Hebrews 9:16-17:

> By introducing the death of the one who made it into his paragraph, the writer of Hebrews has just defined the New Covenant as being a last will and testament rather than being an agreement between God and man. But the New Covenant described by Jeremiah (31:31-33) using the word brit is not a testament or will left by a dead person. It is an agreement, a covenant between God and his chosen one, people. The writer has switched the meanings to make a Hebrew covenant into a Greek will and testament.[8]

Here is how Trimm responds to this charge:

> Hebrews does not refer to a last will and testament, but to inheritance rules related to the ancient Jewish custom of making a blood covenant. When two people entered into a blood covenant, they became members of each other's house including heirship rights. There are two great examples of the making of such a covenant in the Tanak. The first is to be found in Genesis 31:43-54 (between Ya'akov and Lavan). It was through his blood covenant with Jonathan that David inherited the throne of Saul. David had a covenant with Jonathan making him Jonathan's joint heir, when Saul and Jonathan died in the same battle, David inherited the throne. In

the same way we have a covenant with the Son of
the King, when the son of the king died, we were
his joint heirs.

This inheritance is the theme of the Book
of Hebrews. Paul's topic is the Blood Covenant
and inheritance. He shows that the Messiah was
"made heir of all things" (1:2, 4) and the "firstborn"
(1:6; 12:23). He shows that the oath which made
Abraham's seed the chosen people was a covenant
(6:13-14) and that the oath which makes the
Messiah a priest after the order of Melchizedec
(7:20-22) is the renewal of the covenant (Hebrews
7:22; 8:6-13).[9]

But by far, the greatest problem he has with Hebrews is
that he finds the author to be "antinomian" (against the law).
He denigrates the writer as not being "pro-Torah." For example,
quoting the seventh chapter and the twelfth verse, which reads
"for the priesthood being changed, there is made of necessity a
change also of the law," he states that in the original Hebrew
version of the letter, the word translated "change" in Hebrew is
"shenishtana," which means "to repeat, to do a second time." Thus
the HRM version reads: "It is saying that according to which
there is a repetition of the office of the priesthood, of necessity it
is saying there is a repetition of the Torah."

In other words (according to Judah), the verse has nothing to
do with any commandment of the Torah being *changed* but rather
being *repeated*. This, according to Monte Judah and other HRM
teachers, is the primary meaning of this passage in Hebrews.

But such a view does away with the meaning of the verse as
well as the entire argument of the writer in chapters seven and
eight. The argument in those chapters is that you cannot change

the priesthood without changing the law since the Levitical priesthood was instituted under the Mosaic covenant. To change the priesthood, therefore, is to change the law. That's why the writer introduces the need for a New Covenant in chapter eight.

The same is true in chapter 8:13, which clearly states in the King James Version (KJV), "In that he saith, A new covenant, he hath made the first old. Now that which decayeth and waxeth old is ready to vanish away" (Hebrews 8:13, KJV).

Any straight reading of the text makes it clear that the writer is saying that the inaugurating of a New Covenant made the first covenant obsolete. What does the mention of the Old Covenant being ready to vanish away mean? It is no doubt a reference to the fact that the temple was soon to disappear (which indicates a pre-AD 70 writing of this letter). God was about to remove that which was decaying and waxing old forever. This is why the events of AD 70 are part of salvation history. The New Covenant was not firmly in place until the last vestige of the Old Covenant was removed.

What Rejecting Hebrews Means

In order for a book to be accepted into the New Testament canon, it had to be written by an apostle or under the auspices of an apostle. Since no one could say for sure who wrote the book of Hebrews, it struggled long and hard to gain admission into the canon. The earliest authorities attributed it to Paul, but since no one could be sure who wrote it, it was not immediately accepted into the canon.

What won the day for its full acceptance? Even though no one could say for sure whether it was written by an apostle or under the auspices of an apostle, the early church fathers had to admit that it was the most apostolic piece of literature in the entire New Testament! No other book sets forth the Messiah as

God's final Word to mankind in the fashion Hebrews does. And that means that everything which preceded Him was preparatory of what was coming when He arrived.

When seeing what lengths Monte Judah and other HRM teachers will go to discredit the book of Hebrews, it becomes obvious they are dismissing it, not because it was Greek in origin, but due to its content. Hebrews does away with the premise of much of what the HRM is built on. In calling the law a "shadow of the good things to come instead of the true form of these realities," the writer of Hebrews is establishing that the former covenant was preparatory, awaiting fulfillment at the dawning of the new. Now that it has come, the old must now be interpreted in the light of the new.

Monte Judah's refusal to do so (and therefore his rejection of Hebrews as canonical) is more than a hermeneutical error—it's heretical. To reject a book outright as the authoritative Word of God in the light of two thousand years of church history, which views it as such is no light matter. But as we have seen in a previous chapter, HRM teachers have done the same thing with Galatians. Perhaps they have not rejected its canonicity outright, but they have dismissed its content by suggesting that Paul isn't dealing in the letter with written law, but so-called "oral" law.

Looking Ahead

The book of Hebrews contains God's final word for mankind. It sums up fifteen hundred years of Hebrew history, setting forth all that God spoke through the prophets in the Old Testament as being fulfilled in Jesus the Messiah.

Many HRM teachers negate the validity of the book of Hebrews, despite the fact that it gained acceptance as canonical through a long, arduous process. Nevertheless, they reject it simply because it negates the basic presuppositions of the HRM.

They don't accept the New Testament apostolic interpretation of the Old Testament. Instead of believing that the Old Testament should be interpreted in the light of the New, they believe that the New should be interpreted in the light of the Old.

We are now entering the final section of this book entitled "Protecting the Flock." This section, while helpful for all, is primarily written with leaders in mind to whom the responsibility to watch over the flock so as to protect them from error has been given. Chapter 15, "Kill the Spider Before the Eggs Hatch," focuses on how leaders must be diligent to safeguard the flock from HRM influence before it is too late. In the final chapter, "The Only Safeguard: Preaching the Gospel," we will discuss the only true safeguard to protect the people of God from HRM error (and any error)—*having the Gospel of the grace of God laid well as a foundation for the local church*. As it has been said before, the best offense is a good defense. People who are well-grounded in the true Gospel will best be protected from the errors of the HRM.

SECTION 5

Protecting the Flock

CHAPTER 15

Kill the Spider
Before the Eggs Hatch

The title for this chapter is derived from a saying which became popular in a local church where I once served as an elder. The saying was, "It is better to kill the spider before the eggs hatch." It was a euphemism for the importance of dealing with problems when they first surface before they have a chance to morph into major issues. Good leaders learn to spot potential problems and address them before they get out of hand.

The euphemism fits well the burden of the remaining two chapters of this book. Leaders must act decisively and be on the alert if they are to safeguard their flocks from aberrant HRM teaching. One of the major reasons God sets elders in a flock is to safeguard his people from error. The apostle Paul reminds the Ephesian elders that they should always be on their guard so as to not allow error to be taught in the church:

> Pay careful attention to yourselves and to all the flock, in which the Holy Spirit has made you overseers, to care for the church of God, which he obtained with his own blood. I know that after my departure fierce wolves will come in among you, not sparing the flock; and from among your own selves

will arise men speaking twisted things, to draw
away the disciples after them. Therefore be alert,
remembering that for three years, I did not cease
night or day to admonish every one with tears.

— Acts 20:28-31

This is especially important when it comes to HRM teaching
and teachers. I have seen firsthand the damage HRM teachings
and teachers can do when elders aren't diligent to watch over
their flocks. One church I know which failed to deal early with
HRM teachers paid a steep price for their passivity. The damage
was far worse than it should have been had the leaders acted
quickly and decisively.

These two chapters are written to assist leaders in protecting
God's people from unbiblical HRM teaching and teachers. In
this chapter, we will deal with how to detect these errors early
when they arise in a local church. The final chapter will address
the ultimate deterrent against error; properly preaching and
teaching the biblical Gospel.

Recognizing Their M.O.

One of the most helpful things leaders can do to protect their
flocks from unhealthy HRM teaching is to understand HRM
teachers' Mode of Operation (M.O.). By being acquainted with
the way they operate, leaders can be better prepared to react
when their members are being assaulted by HRM teachers.

It is impossible to stereotype how all HRM teachers operate,
yet there are enough similarities to recognize a pattern most
HRM teachers follow. This predictable pattern is described by
the apostle Jude in his short letter:

> For certain people have *crept in unnoticed* who long ago were designated for this condemnation, ungodly people, who pervert the grace of our God into sensuality and deny our only Master and Lord, Jesus Christ.
>
> — Jude 4 (italics mine)

Jude refers to the stealth with which false teachers enter the Church in order to deceive the saints. In Jesus' own words, they come in "sheep's clothing." When applied to HRM teachers, it means they come at first as those desirous of helping others discover the Hebraic roots of the faith. Drawing people into studying with them, these teachers often start by convincing them that the origins of the Christian holidays (Christmas and Easter) are pagan. They then introduce them to the Jewish feasts as a replacement for the Christian holidays. It stands to reason that in order to offer God acceptable worship, they should abandon the pagan holidays for the biblical ones. It is only a matter of time before they are convinced to keep the whole Law along with the Hebrew feasts, including weekly Sabbath observance.

A year or two ago, I received a voicemail from an old friend that I hadn't spoken to in quite a while. In the message he left on my phone, he told me that he had now found the truth. While I was expecting him to say it was faith in Jesus of Nazareth as the Messiah, the truth he had discovered was that God now wanted him to keep the Sabbath and the Jewish feasts. No longer was Yeshua (Jesus) the truth, but living a Jewish lifestyle.

Most Gentiles who first come under this teaching do not immediately abandon their local churches. But eventually, their attendance begins to wane as they realize God has called them to worship on the true Sabbath (Saturday). By planting seeds of doubt regarding their church practices, these Gentile believers eventually find it untenable to continue attending their churches since they are now persuaded that they are steeped in pagan practices.

In the remainder of this chapter, we will look at three characteristics most HRM teachers exhibit when it comes to influencing Gentile believers towards HRM teaching. We already looked at the first one briefly in this chapter. It is that they come with *stealth*, which is another way of saying they come secretly, hiding their true motives. The second is that they come as *independent* agents, acting on their own and under no authority. And finally, they use the law *unlawfully*. Let us look briefly at each one.

THEY COME WITH STEALTH

Since we briefly looked at this one at the beginning of this chapter, I'll just make a few comments about it. Merriam-Webster dictionary defines stealth as "the act or action of proceeding furtively, secretly, or imperceptibly." One acting stealthily is one who hides his or her true motives from others. That is true of how many HRM teachers operate; they hide their true motives under the guise of simply wanting to teach Gentiles the Hebrew roots of the faith. But their real motive is to bring people back under the Law. Remember how the apostle spoke about the false brethren who secretly infiltrated the Galatian churches: "Yet because of false brothers *secretly brought in*—who *slipped in* to spy out our freedom that we have in Jesus, so that they might bring us into slavery" (Galatians 2:4; italics mine).

Notice how Paul describes these people as "false brothers secretly brought in" and that they "slipped in to spy out our freedom." This is how many HRM teachers come into local churches, preying on unsuspecting church members. Since there are so many Gentiles who wish to learn about the Jewish roots of the faith, they are often unaware of their stealth and easily succumb to it. As Paul says in Galatians, they came in this way not to liberate but to bring them into slavery. That is their true motive. They want to bring people back again under the yoke of the law as slaves.

We must be careful not to lump everyone teaching Jewish roots in the same boat. Not everyone is doing it from wrong motives. This became clear to me when I first began teaching Old Testament studies in a local church many years ago. I was astonished at the low level of understanding most believers had of the Hebrew Scriptures. They may know a few of the basic stories, such as David and Goliath, Noah's flood, and the three Hebrew children, but beyond that, they understand very little of its scope. Therefore, there is a great need today to teach believers the Old Testament. In fact, teaching it properly is one of the best safeguards against the temptation to fall for unbiblical HRM teaching.

This differs greatly from why many HRM teachers are teaching the Old Testament. Instead of providing Gentile believers with a foundational understanding of the Hebrew Bible so as to be able to more fully grasp the New, they have as their aim to bring them back into bondage. So while there is a legitimate need to teach the Hebrew Bible in the Church today, the motive of many HRM teachers is not to provide such a foundational understanding in the Scriptures so as to better understand the New Covenant.

THEY ARE UNDER NO AUTHORITY

There is an important statement in the letter the Jerusalem apostles wrote to the Gentiles after the Jerusalem conference. It is a reference to the Judaizers who sought to bring the Gentiles under the bondage of the Law. The apostles called attention to the fact that these false teachers were acting independently when they came from Jerusalem: "Since we have heard that some persons have gone out from us and troubled you with words, unsettling your minds, *although we gave them no instructions*" (Acts 15:24; italics mine).

Do you see what they were saying? The letter makes it clear that these men were not authorized from the Jerusalem church to teach these things. Since they were under no authority, they were acting entirely on their own. The same can be said today of many HRM teachers. Most of these teachers are not authorized to speak what they teach from any credible congregation or sent from any local church eldership. And with the advent of the Internet and social media, anyone can "teach and produce videos without the usual local controls that keep immature and even unknowledgeable believers out of traditional teaching positions."[1] Dawn goes on to recognize the problem:

> Here's the problem: unlike Christianity and
> Judaism, we are a movement largely without a safety
> net in place for new people. Most folks have no
> chance at a local congregation; they have nowhere
> to be nurtured and loved through these difficult first
> few years. As a result, we cannot help but become
> a movement of radically individualized people who
> operate as islands on social media. No support, no
> accountability, no guidance, and oftentimes no real
> growth of anything except anger and resentment.[2]

Notice how Dawn describes the movement as "a movement of radically individualized people who operate as islands on social media." In other words, they are "self-authorized." And because of social media, they can garner an immediate following. Few ask any questions of HRM teachers such as What congregation do you come from? or Who are the elders you are submitted to, and who sent you?

This is a problem, not only when it comes to dealing with the HRM but with other heresies as well. As a local church pastor, it has become painfully real to me that the people I pastor were listening to many different voices during the week before they came to listen to me on Sunday. I got in the habit of reminding my congregation to make sure they were getting their doctrine from their local elders and judging everything else they were hearing in the light of what their elders were telling them. Many of God's people reverse this order, getting their doctrine from the Internet and challenging their elders by what they are hearing outside their local church.

If people followed that advice, it would greatly reduce the influence of HRM teachers since, more than any other movement, it is largely fueled by social media. The airwaves and Internet are filled today with self-appointed teachers who garner a hearing simply because they sound remotely credible. Many of these self-appointed teachers would no doubt say that God authorized them to teach. But it is clear from the New Testament that all true ministry raised up by God is first authenticated and affirmed in the local church. It was the local church at Antioch that laid hands on Paul and Barnabas and "sent them off" (Acts 13:1-4). The call came from God, but the local church at Antioch affirmed it.

That is not the case with many HRM teachers. Few are submitted to local elders who have tested what they are teaching in the rigors of genuine church life. People should ask these teachers who sent them and where they got their authority to teach these things. If they can't answer that question, they are self-appointed teachers and should not be given a hearing. Those who claim to be sent by God should also have a local assembly from whom they are commissioned.

THEY USE THE LAW UNLAWFULLY
(1 TIMOTHY 1:8)

Paul points out in this passage that there are teachers who are "desiring to be teachers of the law without understanding what they are saying or the things of which they make confident assertions" (1 Timothy 1:7). But then he makes the incredible statement: "Now we know that the law is good, if one uses it lawfully" (1 Timothy 1:8). To clarify that statement, he follows it through with the following statement;

> understanding this, that the law is not laid down for
> the just but for the lawless and disobedient, for the
> ungodly and sinners, for the unholy and profane,
> for those who strike their fathers and mothers,
> for murderers, the sexually immoral, men who
> practice homosexuality, enslavers, liars, perjurers,
> and whatever else is contrary to sound doctrine,
> in accordance with the Gospel of the glory of the
> blessed God with which I have been entrusted.
>
> — 1 Timothy 1:9-11

In other words, they use the law *unlawfully*. How? By failing to understand *who* the law is for and why it had been given. The purpose of the law was to convict sinners of their sin; it was not given to the righteous. It is "not laid down for the just"; those already made righteous through Christ. The law has done its work when it convicts us of our sin and drives us to the Messiah for cleansing. This is the proper usage of the law by believers.

David Stern, translator of the Jewish New Testament, listed the following misuses of the Torah:

"(1) Requiring Gentiles to observe aspects of the Torah that were meant only for Jews (Acts 15, 21; Ga 2:11-6:16; Co 2:16-23).

(2) Supposing that mere possession of the Torah guarantees personal salvation (Ro 2:17-3:31, 8:3; MJ 7:11-19).

3) Regarding humanly determined traditions as more authoritative than God's Word itself (Mt 15:1-20, Mk 7:1-23).

(4) Ignoring the New Testament's contribution to the understanding of the Torah (Mt 5:17-20, MJ 8:6).

(5) Using the Torah to lead people away from Yeshua instead of toward him, which is its purpose (Ro 10:4).

(6) Using the Torah as ground for boasting (Ro 3:27-31).

(7) Perverting the Torah into a legalistic system (Ro 3:19-26; Ga 2:16, 3:23)."

Number one is being done repeatedly by many HRM teachers today. Number two was essentially a "Jewish" thing, often carried over to Gentiles who come under HRM teaching. Merely possessing the Torah has nothing to do with personal salvation. As Paul clearly states in Romans, the Jewish people, while counting themselves blessed for possessing the law, were condemned for not keeping it. Number three is indicative of much of Judaism from Jesus' day to today. Jesus regularly dealt with it when he confronted Jewish leaders during his earthly ministry, who had allowed their traditions to become as authoritative as the Word of God.

Chapter 13 deals with number four. The failure to embrace an "apostolic hermeneutic" has meant that instead of interpreting the Old in the light of the New, many are interpreting the New in the light of the Old. This inevitably leads to number five; it is unavoidable under those circumstances. Number six always follows when the Law is not used lawfully. I believe that much HRM teaching instructs Gentiles to boast in the Law.

Number seven is also inevitable, even among those who purpose not to be legalistic. The Torah begins to be viewed as a stepladder to God; the more a person keeps, the more they feel themselves to be in right relationship with God. There has been much written of late pushing back against the idea that first-century Judaism was a legalistic religion. But based on Jesus' interactions with Jewish leaders of his day, the apostle Paul's teaching, especially in the twin books of Romans and Galatians, leads to the conclusion that first-century Judaism was indeed a "works-based" religion.

Looking Ahead

Becoming familiar with how most HRM teachers operate can help leaders to be adequately prepared to shield their people from error. There is a lot more that could be said in this regard, but these three things will suffice in adequately preparing leaders to be on guard against unbiblical Hebrew Roots teaching.

But the ultimate way to safeguard the people of God from doctrinal error is by making sure they are well-founded in the Gospel. Error will have a difficult time finding an audience where people are not only saved by the Gospel but continue to grow and mature in it as well. In the final chapter, we will look carefully at the ultimate safeguard leaders have—properly preaching the biblical Gospel.

CHAPTER 16

Safeguarding the Church Through Gospel Preaching

The previous chapter emphasized that leaders have a special responsibility when it comes to protecting their flocks from doctrinal error. One of the most important functions of local church elders is to exercise oversight so as to protect the flock from aberrant teachings and rogue teachers. While that includes such things as prayer and pastoral ministry, none compares with the responsibility they carry to properly preach and teach the biblical gospel. Indeed, it is the most important weapon in the pastoral toolbox in safeguarding the church from error. This final chapter looks carefully at this matter.

Why is preaching and teaching the biblical gospel one of the most important tools in the pastoral toolbox for guarding the church from the HRM error? Earlier in this book, I mentioned how Secret Service agents are trained to spot counterfeit currency: They study authentic currency so as to become so familiar with it, they are able to immediately spot counterfeit currency when they see it. The same is true for believers in the local church. The more they are exposed to the biblical gospel, the easier it is for them to spot the counterfeit when they see it. For that reason, churches whose leaders take seriously the need to preach and teach the biblical gospel are best suited to prepare God's people to recognize false teaching when they encounter it.

Of course, even sitting under sound doctrine does not automatically guarantee people will be safeguarded from such teaching. The Galatian believers heard the Gospel from none other than the apostle Paul yet still embraced false teaching when they sat under the teaching of the Judaizers. There is no guarantee that even sitting under the biblical Gospel will safeguard us from deception. Nevertheless, those who are given a good foundation in the Gospel have the best chance of staying free from error.

This final chapter deals practically with how leaders can ground the people they serve in the biblical Gospel so as to safeguard them from error of any type, especially the error of aberrant HRM teaching. There is simply no replacement for leaders preaching the Gospel properly to protect God's people from doctrinal error. In this chapter, I address four major aspects of preaching and teaching leaders must be engaged in if they are to take seriously the call to protect their flocks. They are (not in order of importance): (1) the necessity of preaching Christ alone; (2) preaching Jesus from the Hebrew Bible; (3) preaching which contains both continuity and discontinuity; (4) and pursuing an expository ministry.

Make Your Preaching and Teaching About Jesus

The Gospel, in its essence, is about the Lord Jesus Christ—His Person and work on behalf of guilty sinners. Therefore, the most important thing leaders can do is to make sure their teaching and preaching are centered in the Person of Jesus Christ. The Gospel is not about the plan of salvation but about the glorious

Person of the Son of God. In a word, Jesus is the Gospel! Paul, in his letter to the Romans, starts with this description of the Gospel:

> Paul, a servant of Christ Jesus, called to be an apostle, set apart for the Gospel *of God*, which he promised beforehand through his prophets in the holy Scriptures, *concerning his Son*, who was descended from David according to the flesh and was declared to be the Son of God in power according to the Spirit of holiness by his resurrection from the dead, Jesus Christ our Lord.
>
> — Romans 1:1-4 (italics mine)

According to the apostle Paul, the Gospel is the "gospel of God." By that phrase, he means that it both came *from* God and is centered *in* the person of God. No one but God could have come up with the Gospel. But it is also true that the Gospel is centered in the Person of his Son, whom Paul describes as both having been descended from David according to his human nature and declared to be the Son of God by his glorious resurrection from the dead (Romans 1:3-4). Paul takes the remaining chapters in his letter to unpack what the Father accomplished through the Son in redeeming sinful humanity.

When we say that the Gospel is about a *Person*, we are referring both to who He is in His essential nature, as well as what He accomplished on our behalf by consenting to become a human being, living as a Man for thirty-three years, dying for sin, and rising from the dead to justify His claims. When we are engaged in preaching and teaching the biblical Gospel, we will be focused on both of these. We will not be presenting a program or a plan but a glorious Person Who is the Foundation upon which everything is built (1 Corinthians 3:10-11). Just as the foundation of a building determines the strength of the structure built upon it, so also the foundation of Jesus must be carefully laid in people's lives. As the apostle Peter reminds us, He is the "stone which the builders rejected that has now become the cornerstone (1 Peter 2:9). According to Merriam- Webster, the cornerstone is "a stone forming a part of a corner or angle in a wall" (Merriam- Webster, Cornerstone).

I remember a particular time early in my ministry when God led me to examine the substance of what I had been preaching and teaching. I was shocked to discover how little I had preached Christ and how much of my teaching was moralistic. I was deeply repentant and, from that moment on, made a commitment to a more Christ-centered ministry.

Paul essentially describes his own ministry as preaching "Christ crucified" (1 Corinthians 1:23). Even a cursory reading of 1 Corinthians reveals how Christ-centered he was. In that letter, he answered several doctrinal questions concerning things such as food offered to idols, marriage and divorce, and the gifts of the Spirit. Nevertheless, the name *Jesus* or *Lord Jesus* appears over and over again, even when dealing with these various topics. As the spokes of a bicycle wheel all meet in the center, the Lord Jesus Christ is the Center in which all the spokes of Christian truth meet.

Preaching and teaching the Lord Jesus Christ has practical results in the life of the people of God, not the least of which is that people who are continually satisfied with Jesus will not feel the need to look for something else. I am convinced that many people get caught up in these spiritual tangents simply because they are not satisfied in Christ. According to the book of Hebrews, Jesus is so much *better* than anything religion has to offer. When people are satisfied with Christ, they are not likely to feel the need to look elsewhere.

Teach and Preach Jesus
from the Hebrew Bible

One of the best safeguards against the incursion of extreme HRM teaching into a local assembly is to teach and preach Jesus from the pages of the Hebrew Bible. This accomplishes at least two things. First, we are imitating our Lord Himself, Who, as previously seen, took His disciples through a whirlwind tour of each of the three divisions of the Hebrew Bible, demonstrating how He is the interpretive key (Luke 24:25-26, Luke 24:44-47). It is wonderful indeed to follow our Lord in this endeavor of making Himself known in the pages of the Old Testament.

Too many leaders today shrink back from the challenge of teaching the Hebrew Bible in their churches, which has resulted in God's people being unfamiliar with it. They may know some of its main stories, such as the flood of Noah, David and Goliath, and Daniel in the lion's den, but they do not have a firm grasp on the flow of biblical history and its significance. Their view of the Old Testament is often moralistic; David and Goliath is about faith, Daniel—courage, Jonah—obedience, etc. But such handling of the Word of God keeps people from grasping the real significance of the Scriptures in terms of the coming of the Messiah. And this contributes greatly to the temptation for people to fall prey to extreme HRM teaching.

Besides imitating our Lord, the second benefit to regularly preaching and teaching through the Old Testament is that it allows us to interpret the Old Testament in the light of the New. We looked at this briefly back in chapter fourteen. By giving people the interpretive key, we protect them from those who would insist that the New Testament should be interpreted in the light of the Old rather than the Old in the light of the New. By so doing, we ensure that people are well-grounded in the Old Testament. This is a buffer against aberrant HRM teachings.

Over the years, I have regularly taught on the Hebrew feasts in the churches I have worked with. To this day, these teachings remain some of the most requested series in our teaching library. But what I teach about the feasts is radically different from what most HRM teachers teach. I do not teach them because I desire for believers to observe them in place of the Christian holidays but as a means of illuminating the New Covenant. In other words, they serve as part of the elaborate shadow language God gave in the Old Testament to prepare the world for the coming of the Messiah and the dawning of the New Covenant. I am not trying to convince Gentiles to keep these feasts *literally* but to help them to become more acquainted with how these feasts foreshadowed the realities which were to come in the Messiah.

Jesus Himself demonstrated how the feasts were part of the elaborate shadow language of the Old Testament in a story John records in the seventh chapter of his Gospel. Jesus was in Jerusalem, observing the Feast of Tabernacles in early Autumn. That feast followed the ingathering of the crops into the barns. It was the most joyous of the feasts being known as the "season of our rejoicing." The harvest was gathered, and now the people of Israel were invited to rejoice in his goodness displayed throughout the year. For seven days, the people were commanded to live in booths made of leaves and branches, celebrating with joy, dancing, singing, and shouting (see Leviticus 23:40).

On the seventh day, the final day of the feast, there was a special celebration. The priest would send a celebrant with a branch of a myrtle tree, one from a willow, and another with a palm tree all tied together in his right hand. He also carried citrus branches bound together in his left hand. One of the priests would carry in his hand a golden pitcher and would lead the crowd in procession to the accompaniment of flutes and trumpets to the pool of Siloam. Once there, he would fill the pitcher with water from the pool and then lead the worshippers back to the temple. Author Sam Storms highlights what happened afterwards:

> He immediately proceeded to the altar where the sacrifice had been offered and there poured the water into a funnel which led to the base of the altar. Then, to the accompaniment of the flute, shaking the lulabha in the right hand and the throng in the left, all the people would chant, antiphonally, Psalm 113-118, climaxed by the public recitation of Psalm 118:24-29. The symbolic purpose of the water ritual considered the high point of the festival, was to remind the people of the provision of water from God during the time of wilderness wandering (see Num. 20:7-11;) as well as his showering the earth to make possible the growth of their crops.[1]

It is in the seventh chapter of John's Gospel we learn that at the moment this ritual was being performed, a young Nazarene stood and cried out, "If anyone thirsts, let him come to me and drink. Whoever believes in me, as the Scripture has said, 'Out of his heart will flow rivers of living water'" (John 7:37b-38).

By this proclamation, the Messiah declared that this feast was ultimately about Him. He was the One who fulfilled the promise by giving the Spirit to those who believe. That water ritual embodied the promised pouring out of the Spirit when the Messiah came. That feast has its ultimate fulfillment in Jesus, Who gives the Spirit freely.

It is imperative, therefore, that leaders learn to preach the Gospel through the pages of the Old Testament. By so doing, they lower the chances of people falling prey to false teachings. It also contributes greatly to helping people understand key books of the New Testament, such as Revelation, which depends so heavily on the Old Testament for its understanding. I myself have found a great eagerness in most non-Jewish believers to learn the Old Testament. Sadly, few find churches today where the Old Testament is regularly being taught. Because this void is not being filled by sound teaching of church leaders, it is easily filled by those teaching false doctrine.

The challenge I want to issue to those responsible for the ministry of the word in their churches is to be proactive in regularly preaching through the Old Testament. That means, of course, that they will have to spend considerable time immersed in the stories and the theological propositions of the Hebrew Bible if they want to be proficient in teaching it in their churches. But if they are willing to do so, it shall reap a rich reward in shielding people from the errors of much HRM teaching.

Demonstrate Both Continuity and Discontinuity in Preaching

In theology, two terms often used to describe the relationship between the Old and New Testaments are *continuity* and *discontinuity*. Together, they answer the question: What things from the Old are continued in the New and which things are not? Without overgeneralizing, it seems to me that this lies at the heart of understanding how the HRM deals with the relationship between the Testaments. Many HRM teachers see only continuity between them and not discontinuity. But the truth is, wherever true Gospel preaching occurs, there will be both continuity and discontinuity. Let me explain.

The fact that there is continuity between the Testaments is evident in the fact that it is the same God whose nature and attributes are revealed in both (see Hebrews 1:1-3). This is vital to grasp. I once had someone tell me that it seemed to them as if we actually switched Gods at Calvary—that the God of the Old Testament was wrathful and vengeful, while the God of the New Testament seemed gracious and merciful, having been softened by Jesus Christ. While I know what this person was trying to say, this can't be supported at all by Scripture. The truth is, the same God is revealed in both Testaments. In fact, the revelation of God found in the Hebrew Bible is the foundation of all that is revealed in the New Testament. The God of Israel is the God of both Testaments. The approach towards Him has changed, but it is the same God Who is being approached.

It is true that God was wrathful in the Old Testament, as evidenced by such events as the Flood and the destruction of Sodom and Gomorrah. But that does not mean his wrath is not also demonstrated in the New Testament. When Ananias and his wife Sapphira lied about the money they had given after selling a property, the Spirit revealed it to Peter, who subsequently confronted them. God executed each one on the spot for their deception (Acts 5:1-11). Paul also was used by God to inflict blindness on a false prophet who tried to hinder a government official from hearing the Gospel (Acts 13:4-12). So the idea that there were no displays of wrath in the New Testament is just not true.

In the same way, even though it wasn't until the dawning of the New Covenant that men and women knew the full power of justifying grace, men and women knew justification under the Old Covenant as well. Even after sinning by taking another man's wife and arranging for her husband's death, David speaks of the blessing on the "one whose transgression is forgiven, whose sin is covered. Blessed is the man against whom the Lord counts no iniquity, and in whose spirit there is no deceit" (Psalm 32:1-2). David deserved both death and divine judgment, but he received neither because of God's forgiving grace. Is this not the New Testament doctrine of justification?

Another aspect of continuity between the Testaments is that the people of God of both testaments are constituted such on the basis of covenant. Israel became the people of God based on the covenant God made with them at Sinai (Exodus 19-12). So also, the people of God in the New Testament are such on the basis of a covenant that God made with them (Matthew 26:28, Hebrews 8:6-7). This New Covenant is enacted on better promises and therefore is a better covenant. But it simply underscores the fact that without covenant, the people of God would not exist.

But if there is much continuity between the testaments when it comes to the people of God, there is also much discontinuity. For one, there is a fundamental change in the national character of the people of God from a predominantly Jewish community to one predominantly Gentile. The book of Acts records how, as the Gospel traveled westward; it was believed on largely by Gentiles. Paul demonstrates in Romans 11 that it was according to the divine plan that the majority of Jews be hardened, except for a remnant (Romans 11:7-10). The people of God are now not such on the basis of nationality but on the basis of faith in the Gospel. While a remnant of Jews will still believe in every generation, most of those who believe will be Gentiles. The Church of God is now an international community, constituted by personal faith in Jesus as the Messiah.

There is also a change in the administration of the kingdom of God. It has been taken away from Israel after the flesh and now given to the Church (Matthew 21:43). Previously, Gentiles were excluded from the commonwealth of Israel and could only be joined to Israel by means of circumcision. But now, circumcision means nothing, having been rendered obsolete by the new creation (Galatians 6:15). Therefore, Gentiles who believe are joined to their Jewish counterparts in the "one new man" (Ephesians 2:15). No outward mark, but only the inward work of the Spirit has joined them to the Israel of God (Galatians 6:16). The ordinances of the two covenants have changed as well, from circumcision in the Old to baptism and the Lord's Supper in the New. No longer is the earmark that one belongs to the people of God an outward mark in the flesh, but possession of the Spirit producing the fruit of his presence (Galatians 5:22-23).

Leaders must preach and teach both continuity and discontinuity if they are to remain faithful to the Gospel. Things like the feasts, the Sabbath, and the dietary laws must be placed in the discontinuous category, while the nature of God and the need for covenant as the basis for peoplehood are continuous. By making this clear in our preaching and teaching, we will insure that God's people avoid extreme HRM teaching, which downplays or ignores the reality of discontinuity entirely.

Pursue an Expository Ministry

The false teaching of many HRM teachers is not unlike that of another false teaching in that it is built on texts wrenched out of their context. But as the saying goes, "a text without a context is a pretext." Many cults such as Jehovah's Witnesses are experts at this. Sadly, so are many HRM teachers.

What is the best safeguard against this? It is to exercise an expository teaching ministry in the local church. What is expository preaching? "Expository preaching is a form of preaching that details the meaning of a particular text or passage of Scripture" (Expository Preaching, Wikipedia). In other words, it is preaching and teaching, which allows the meaning of the text to govern the sermon. Much preaching today, while claiming to be expository, really isn't. I have often referred to it as "state your text and depart ye from it." Listening to some preaching today, I wonder why the preacher even bothered to have a text. While he occasionally landed back on the text, it is obvious that the text clearly didn't govern the sermon.

Preaching, which allows the Bible itself to speak, accomplishes several things. For one, people are exposed to the Scriptures rather than the thoughts of a man, which builds respect for the authority of Scripture. When leaders handle the Scriptures properly, people gain a new appreciation for the Bible, and that, in turn, creates a hunger to grow in the knowledge of Scripture. When people experience the burning heart the two on the road to Emmaus did, they will keep coming back for more (Luke 24:32). I have sat under Bible exposition that made me wish it would never end. On the other hand, I have sat under preaching where I experienced Hebrews 12:19: "those who heard begged that no further word be spoken" (Hebrews 12:19b, NASB).

While I regularly practice expository preaching, I admit having a "love/hate relationship" to it. I love it because I get to focus on studying the passage I am preaching from rather than spend the majority of my time each week trying to figure out from what text to preach. At the same time, I hate it (not really) because it forces me to have to deal with texts I usually am tempted to ignore. But that's the beauty of preaching through books of Scripture—you get to preach the text as God originally meant it.

I remember the first time preaching through the letter to the Hebrews. It was eye-opening both as a Jew and a believer. As a Jew, it made sense of almost two thousand years of Hebrew history. And as a believer in Jesus as the Messiah, it ratified my faith in Him. He was so much "better" than anything under the Old Covenant! Week by week, as I unpacked the riches of grace found in the pages of that majestic letter, my appreciation for the Son of God quadrupled. I owe most of my Christology (theology of Christ) to that letter. As a safeguard against the infiltration of extreme HRM teaching, I heartily recommend that leaders take their churches through a thorough study of this majestic letter. The best offense is a good defense. Seeing how the writer of Hebrews interprets the history, types, laws, rituals, and covenants of the Old Testament will go a long way in safeguarding believers from attraction towards unhealthy HRM teaching. Grounding your people in how first-century apostles handled the Scriptures in this letter will assist greatly in assuring that people discern truth from error.

Healthy Churches Avoid Error

The simple truth that this chapter sets forth is that healthy churches are churches that will not fall for error. Just as the human body maintains health by having the right supply of nutrients and other things within, so the church that is built up through sound doctrine is able to avoid the pitfalls of extreme HRM teaching and other forms of error. Another term for "sound" doctrine is "healthy" doctrine. Healthy churches are churches that "agree with the sound words of our Lord Jesus Christ and the teaching that accords with godliness" (1 Timothy 6:3b). They fulfill Paul's words to Timothy that he "follow the pattern of the sound words that you have heard from me, in the faith and love that are in Christ Jesus." And they have learned to "guard the good deposit entrusted to you" (2 Timothy 1:14b). These verses are a tonic in a day and age when most churches are blasé when it comes to doctrine.

Leaders must take these words (and scores of others like them) to heart by making sure they are feeding their flocks properly. General exhortations to "love Jesus" will not suffice in safeguarding their flocks from error. They must take up the "sword of the Spirit, which is the word of God" (Ephesians 6:17b). In our day, the enemy is on the prowl, seeking whom he may devour (1 Peter 5:8). Leaders must lead by making sure they are feeding their flocks the good word of God, thus fulfilling Peter's command that they "shepherd the flock of God that is among you" (1 Peter 5:2a).

Shepherds must seek church health before church growth. Today, many leaders flock to conferences where they learn principles of how to grow their churches numerically. Teaching sound doctrine is not at the top of the list of things that will guarantee their churches will grow. But here is a simple but powerful reality—*healthy sheep reproduce*. In a flock, it is not the job of shepherds to reproduce. Rather, they must make sure their flocks have the richest pasturelands to feed on so that they will grow and eventually reproduce.

ENDNOTES

Chapter 1

1. "What Is the Hebrew Roots Movement." GotQuestions. org. Accessed March 18, 2018. www.gotquestions?.org.

2. Ibid

3. "British Israelism." Wikipedia. Wikimedia Foundation. Accessed March 4, 2018. https://en.wikipedia.org/wiki/ British_Israelism.

Chapter 2

1. Wilson, Marvin R. "The Root and Branches." *Our Father Abraham: Jewish Roots of the Christian Faith*, 9–10. Grand Rapids, MI: Wm. B. Eerdmans Publishing Co., 1989.

2. Ibid

3. Wilson, Marvin R. "A Neglected Treasure." *Our Father Abraham: Jewish Roots of the Christian Faith*, 110. Grand Rapids, MI: Wm. B. Eerdmans Publishing Co., 1989.

4. Wilson, Marvin R. "The Root and Branches." *Our Father Abraham: Jewish Roots of the Christian Faith*, 7. Grand Rapids, MI: Wm. B. Eerdmans Publishing Co., 1989.

Chapter 3

1. Ditzel, Peter. "Hebraic Movement." Word of His Grace Ministries, 2013. Accessed January 6, 2019. https://www.wordofhisgrace.org.

2. Leiter, Charles. "Chapter 1." *The Law of Christ*. Hannibal, MO: Granted Ministries Press, 2012.

3. Ditzel, Peter. "Hebraic Movement." Word of His Grace Ministries, 2013. Accessed January 6, 2019. https://www.wordofhisgrace.org.

4. Leiter, Charles. "Chapter 1." *The Law of Christ*. Hannibal, MO: Granted Ministries Press, 2012.

Chapter 4

1. Arakaki, Robert. "Constantine the Great: Roman Emperor, Christian Saint, History's Turning Point." Accessed July 10, 2019. http://antiochian.org.

2. Busenitz, Nathan. *"Did Constantine Invent the Trinity?": The Doctrine of the Trinity in the Writings of the Early Church Fathers* MSJ 24/2. Fall 2013ed. Vol. MSJ 24/2. 217-242. Sun Valley, CA: The Master's Seminary, 2013.

3. Stern, David H. "Chapter 15." In *Jewish New Testament Commentary: a Companion Volume to the Jewish New Testament*, 274–74. Clarksville, MD: Jewish New Testament Publications, 1999.

4. Bevere, Allan R, and Don Closson. Trinity Tuesday: Did the Emperor Constantine Impose the Doctrine of the Trinity on the Council of Nicea? May 6, 2014. http://www.allanbevere.com/2014/05/trinity-tuesday-did-emperer-constantine.html.

5. Ibid

Chapter 5

1. Tertullian. "Did the First Christian Believers Keep the Sabbath and If so on Which Day?" Christianity Stack Exchange. De Fuga in Persecutione, XIV, October 1, 1960. https://christianity.stackexchange.com/questions/5333

2. Ignatius. "Ignatius to the Magnesians." St. Ignatius of Antioch to the Magnesians (Lightfoot translation). Chapter 9. Apostolic Fathers Lightfoot & Harmer, 1891 translation. Accessed April 4, 2018. http://www.earlychristianwritings. com/text/ignatius-magnesians-lightfoot.html.

3. Martyr, Justin. "The Apostolic Fathers, and the Apologists, 95-180 A.D." Rev. George A. Jackson, 1881. Martyr Apologies 1:67. EWTN Global Catholic Television Network. Accessed April 4, 2018. https://www.ewtn.com/ catholicism/library/significance-of-st-justin-martyr-10876.

4. Ibid

5. Schaff, Philip. "The Theological Principles Involved: Import of the Controversy Note 1." In *History of the Christian Church: Volume 3: Nicene and Post-Nicene Christianity*, 380. Broken Arrow, OK: Vision for Maximum Impact, 2017.

6. "Quick Q&A: Did the Sabbath Change from the Seventh Day of the Week to the First?" | The Bible Says That.com. Accessed February 2, 2018. https://www.thebiblesaysthat. com/articles/sabbath/quick-qa-did-sabbath-change-seventh-day-week-first.

7. "Constantine Decrees 'Sun-Day' As Day of Rest." Facts and History. History.com. Accessed October 20, 2018. https://

factsandhistory.com/constantine-decrees-sun-day-as-day-of-rest-instead-of-saturday-on-march-7-321/.

8. Clark, R Scott. "Sabbaths or Sabbath in Colossians 2:16." Web log. *The Heidelblog* (blog), November 4, 2014. [Search domain heidelblog.net] https://heidelblog.net/2014/11/sabbaths-or-sabbath-in-colossians-21617/.

9. Leiter, Charles. "Part 1." In *The Law of Christ*. Hannibal, MO: Granted Ministries Press, 2012.

10. Curtis, David B. "The Hebrew Roots Movement – Part 1." https://www.bereanbiblechurch.org, May 11, 2014. https://www.bereanbiblechurch.org/transcripts/colossians/col_02_16-17_hebrew-roots-movement.htm.

Chapter 6

1. Juster, Daniel. "The Danger of Jewish Roots Movements by Daniel Juster." International Coalition of Apostolic Leaders. International Coalition of Apostolic Leaders, July 31, 2019. https://www.icaleaders.com/news/2019/7/22/the-danger-of-jewish-roots-movements-by-daniel-juster.

Chapter 7

1. "December 17, 2013." Green Baggins, December 17, 2013. https://greenbaggins.wordpress.com/2013/12/17/.

Chapter 8

1. Wright, Christopher J. Introduction. In *Knowing Jesus Through the Old Testament: Rediscovering the Roots of Our Faith*, 1-2. Marshall Pickering, 1992.

2. Wright, *Knowing Jesus Through the Old Testament: Rediscovering the Roots of Our Faith*, 2.

3. Saldarini, Anthony J. "Our Ancient Hebrew Roots," April 1, 2012. https://rosemary-bridges.blogspot.com/2012/04/.

4. "If His Name Was Yeshua, Why Do We Call Him Jesus?" GotQuestions.org, September 22, 2013. https://www.gotquestions.org/Yeshua-Jesus.html.

5. Fobbs, Ollie. *Spiritual Gifts and Abilities*. 84. Richmond, VA, 2015.

6. "If His Name Was Yeshua, Why Do We Call Him Jesus?" GotQuestions.org, September 22, 2013. https://www.gotquestions.org/Yeshua-Jesus.html.

7. Telchin, Stan. *Messianic Judaism Is Not Christianity: A Loving Call to Unity*. Grand Rapids, MI: Chosen Books, 2004.

Chapter 9

1. Hegg, Tim. "Hebrew Roots Heresies." Christian Research Service, April 20, 2020. https://www.christianresearchservice.com/hebrew-roots-heresies/.

2. Roberson, Dianne. "What Is the Hebrew Roots Movement?" churchwatchcentral.com, September 23, 2016. https://churchwatchcentral.com/2016/09/23/what-is-the-hebrew-roots-movement/.

3. McWilliams, Glenn. "A Reasonable Argument for Keeping the Torah." Facebook. Accessed February 10, 2018. https://ko-kr.facebook.com/notes/johan-koch/a-reasonable-argument-for-keeping-the-torah-by-glenn-mcwilliams/10154648109523659/.

4. Nison, Paul. "Messianic Judaism/Hebrew Roots." Torah Life Ministries, 2013. http://torahlifeministries.org/messianic/.

5. Sanchez, Steve. "Not to Abolish But to Fulfill" 14. Not to Abolish But to Fulfill (Matthew 5:17-20) | Bible. org. Accessed February 10, 2019. https://bible.org/seriespage/14-not-abolish-fulfill-matthew-517-20.

6. "God's Law Abides!" God's Law Abides!, Matthew 5:17-20: A Sermon Message from Bethany Bible Church, September 19, 2004. http://www.bethanybible.org/archive/2004/091904.htm.

Chapter 10

1. Deem, Rich. "Did Paul Invent Christianity? Is the Founder of the Christian Religion Paul of Tarsus or Jesus of Nazareth?" Did Paul Invent Christianity? Is the Founder of the Christian Religion Paul of Tarsus or Jesus of Nazareth?" March 20, 2010. https://www.godandscience.org/apologetics/paul_invented_christianity.html.

Chapter 11

1. Cotler, Irwin. "What Is the Origin of the Oral Torah?" Israel Drazin | The Blogs, October 27, 2019. https://blogs.timesofisrael.com/what-is-the-origin-of-the-oral-torah.

2. Encyclopedia of Religion. Encyclopedia.com. 15 Apr. 2021." Encyclopedia.com. Encyclopedia.com, April 15, 2021. https://www.encyclopedia.com/environment/encyclopedias-almanacs-transcripts-and-maps/rabbinic-judaism-late-antiquity.

3. Frenkel, Steven. Rabbinic Judaism and the Synagogue, April 18, 2009. https://jewishbeliefs.blogspot.com/2009/04/rabbinic-judaism-and-synagogue.html.

4. Fisher, Richard. "Bewitching Believers Through the Hebrew Roots Movement." Christian Chat Rooms & Forums, December 30, 2013. https://christianchat.com/bible-discussion-forum/bewitching-believers-through-the-hebrew-roots-movement.81654.

5. Fisher, Richard. "Bewitching Believers Through the Hebrew Roots Movement." thebereancall.org, January 2014. https://www.thebereancall.org/content/january-2014-bewitching-believers-hebrew-roots.

6. Lehrer, Steve. "Is There a Future for Israel in Romans 11?" Is There A Future for Israel in Romans 11, https://docplayer.net/20986333-Is-there-a-future-for-israel-in-romans-11-by-steve-lehrer.html

7. Holland, Tim. *The Olive Tree. Facebook.* Berean Bible Church, n.d. https://www.facebook.com/BereanBibleChurch/videos/243541870892741/.

Chapter 12

1. Telchin, Stan. In *"Messianic Judaism Is Not Christianity": A Loving Warning to Believers*, 83. Grand Rapid, MI: Chosen, 2004.

2. Ibid

3. Telchin, Stan. In *"Messianic Judaism Is Not Christianity": A Loving Warning to Believers*, 89-90. Grand Rapid, MI: Chosen, 2004.

Chapter 13

1. "We Don't Need Teachers Addressing Misusage of Scripture in the Hebrew Roots Movement Part 1." churchword.org, February 26, 2016. http://churchword. org/2016/03/02/dont-need-teachers-addressing-misusage-scripture-hrm-pt-3/.

2. Ibid

3. Ibid

4. "Tanach (Jewish Bible)." BJE. Board of Jewish Education, August 26, 2020. https://bje.org.au/knowledge-centre/jewish-texts/tanach/.

5. Lyons, Eric. "Revelation and the Old Testament." ApologeticsPress.org, 2002. https://apologeticspress.org/apcontent.aspx?category=11&article=886.

Chapter 14

1. Hodges, Zane. "Introduction to Hebrews." In *The Bible Knowledge Commentary*, 992. Wheaton, IL: Victor Books, 1983.

2. Judah, Monte. "The Paradigm of the Hebrews." Challenging Monte Judah's assertion that the Book of Hebrews should be tossed, November 2005. https://www.therefinersfire.org/book_of_hebrews.htm.

3. Ibid

4. Home - The Septuagint: LXX. Greek Orthodox Archdiocese of America, n.d. https://www.septuagint.bible/.

5. "Septuagint." Wikipedia. Wikimedia Foundation. Accessed June 5, 2020. https://en.wikipedia.org/wiki/Septuagint.

6. Trimm, James Scott. "In the Defense of the Book of Hebrews." Nazarene Judaism, June 22, 2008. https://nazarenejudaism.com/?page_id=141.

7. Ibid

8. Ibid

9. Ibid

Chapter 15

1. Dawn, Tyler. "Why've So Many Mature Voices From the Hebrew Roots Movement Are Heading Back to the Church." The Ancient Bridge, July 26, 2016. https://theancientbridge.com/2016/07.

2. Stern, David. "Misuses of the Torah." kifakz.github.io. Accessed March 18, 2019. https://kifakz.github.io/eng/bible/stern/stern_1-timofeiu_01.html.

Chapter 16

1. Storms, Sam. In *Kingdom Come: the Amillennial Alternative*: Safeguarding the Church Through Gospel Preaching. 264. Fearn, Scotland: Christian Focus Publications Ltd, 2013.

BIBLIOGRAPHY

Arakaki, Robert. "Constantine the Great: Roman Emperor, Christian Saint, History's Turning Point." Accessed July 10, 2019. http://antiochian.org.

Bevere, Allan R. and Closson, Don. Trinity Tuesday: Did the Emperor Constantine Impose the Doctrine of the Trinity on the Council of Nicea? May 6, 2014. http://www.allanbevere.com/2014/05/trinity-tuesday-did-emperer-constantine.html.

"Bewitching Believers Through the Hebrew Roots Movement." Christian Chat Rooms & Forums, December 30, 2013. https://christianchat.com/bible-discussion-forum/bewitching-believers-through-the-hebrew-roots-movement.81654/.

"British Israelism." Wikipedia. Wikimedia Foundation. Accessed March 4, 2018. https://en.wikipedia.org/wiki/British_Israelism.

Busenitz, Nathan. Rep. *Did Constantine Invent the Trinity?: The Doctrine of the Trinity in the Writings of the Early Church Fathers* MSJ 24/2. Fall 2013ed. Vol. MSJ 24/2. 217-242. Sun Valley, CA: The Master's Seminary, 2013.

Clark, R Scott. "Sabbaths or Sabbath in Colossians 2:16 ." Web log. *The Heidelblog* (blog), November 4, 2014. [Search domain heidelblog.net] https://heidelblog.net/2014/11/sabbaths-or-sabbath-in-colossians-21617/.

Closson, Don. "The Council of Nicea and the Doctrine of the Trinity." Probe Ministries, May 27, 2003. https://probe.org/the-council-of-nicea/.

"Constantine Decrees 'Sun-Day' As Day of Rest." FactsandHistory. History.com. Accessed October 20, 2018. https://factsandhistory.com/constantine-decrees-sun-day-as-day-of-rest-instead-of-saturday-on-march-7-321/.

Cotler, Irwin. "What Is the Origin of the Oral Torah?" Israel Drazin | The Blogs, October 27, 2019. https://blogs.timesofisrael.com/what-is-the-origin-of-the-oral-torah.

Curtis, David B. "The Hebrew Roots Movement - Part 1." https://www.bereanbiblechurch.org, May 11, 2014. https://www.bereanbiblechurch.org/transcripts/colossians/col_02_16-17_hebrew-roots-movement.htm.

Dawn, Tyler. "Why So Many Mature Voices From the Hebrew Roots Movement Are Heading Back to the Church." The Ancient Bridge, July 26, 2016. https://theancientbridge.com/2016/07.

"December 17, 2013." Green Baggins, December 17, 2013. https://greenbaggins.wordpress.com/2013/12/17/.

Deem, Rich. "Did Paul Invent Christianity? Is the Founder of the Christian Religion Paul of Tarsus or Jesus of Nazareth?" Did Paul Invent Christianity? Is the Founder of the Christian Religion Paul of Tarsus or

Jesus of Nazareth? March 20, 2010. https://www.
godandscience.org/apologetics/paul_invented_
christianity.html.

Ditzel, Peter. "Hebraic Movement." Word of His Grace.
Accessed January 6, 2019. https://www.wordofhisgrace.
org.

Encyclopedia of Religion. Encyclopedia.com. 15 Apr. 2021
<https: www.encyclopedia.com="">." Encyclopedia.
com. Encyclopedia.com, April 15, 2021. https://
www.encyclopedia.com/environment/encyclopedias-
almanacs-transcripts-and-maps/rabbinic-judaism-late-
antiquity. </https:>

Fisher, Richard. "Bewitching Believers Through the Hebrew
Roots Movement." thebereancall.org, January 2014.
https://www.thebereancall.org/content/january-2014-
bewitching-believers-hebrew-roots.

Fobbs, Ollie. *Spiritual Gifts and Abilities*. Richmond, VA, 2015.

Frenkel, Steven. Rabbinic Judaism and the Synagogue, April
18, 2009. https://jewishbeliefs.blogspot.com/2009/04/
rabbinic-judaism-and-synagogue.html.

"God's Law Abides!" God's Law Abides!, Matthew 5:17-
20: A Sermon Message from Bethany Bible Church,
September 19, 2004. http://www.bethanybible.org/
archive/2004/091904.htm.

Hegg, Tim. "Hebrew Roots Heresies." Christian
Research Service, April 20, 2020. https://www.
christianresearchservice.com/hebrew-roots-heresies/.

Hodges, Zane. "Introduction to Hebrews." In *The Bible Knowledge Commentary*, 992. Wheaton, IL: Victor Books, 1983.

Holland, Tim. *The Olive Tree. Facebook*. Berean Bible Church, n.d. https://www.facebook.com/BereanBibleChurch/videos/243541870892741/.

Home - The Septuagint: LXX. Greek Orthodox Archdiocese of America, n.d. https://www.septuagint.bible/.

"If His Name Was Yeshua, Why Do We Call Him Jesus?" GotQuestions.org, September 22, 2013. https://www.gotquestions.org/Yeshua-Jesus.html.

Ignatius. "Ignatius to the Magnesians." St. Ignatius of Antioch to the Magnesians (Lightfoot translation). Apostolic Fathers Lightfoot & Harmer, 1891 translation. Accessed April 4, 2018. http://www.earlychristianwritings.com/text/ignatius-magnesians-lightfoot.html.

Judah, Monte. "The Paradigm of the Hebrews." Challenging Monte Judah's assertion that the Book of Hebrews should be tossed, November 2005. https://www.therefinersfire.org/book_of_hebrews.htm.

Juster, Daniel. "The Danger of Jewish Roots Movements by Daniel Juster." International Coalition of Apostolic Leaders. International Coalition of Apostolic Leaders, July 31, 2019. https://www.icaleaders.com/news/2019/7/22/the-danger-of-jewish-roots-movements-by-daniel-juster.

Lehrer, Steve. "Is There a Future for Israel in Romans 11?"
        Is There A Future for Israel in Romans 11, https://
        docplayer.net/20986333-Is-there-a-future-for-israel-in-
        romans-11-by-steve-lehrer.html

Leiter, Charles. "Chapter 1." In *The Law of Christ*. Hannibal,
        MO: Granted Ministries Press, 2012.

Leiter, Charles. "Part 1." In *The Law of Christ*. Hannibal, MO:
        Granted Ministries Press, 2012.

Lyons, Eric. "Revelation and the Old Testament."
        ApologeticsPress.org, 2002. https://apologeticspress.
        org/apcontent.aspx?category=11&article=886.

Martyr, Justin. "'The Apostolic Fathers, and the Apologists,
        95-180 A.D." EWTN Global Catholic Television
        Network. Accessed April 4, 2018. https://www.ewtn.
        com/catholicism/library/significance-of-st-justin-
        martyr-10876.

McWilliams, Glenn. "A Reasonable Argument for Keeping
        the Torah." Facebook. Accessed February 10, 2018.
        https://ko-kr.facebook.com/notes/johan-koch/a-
        reasonable-argument-for-keeping-the-torah-by-glenn-
        mcwilliams/10154648109523659/.

Nison, Paul. "Messianic Judaism/Hebrew Roots." Torah
        Life Ministries, 2013. http://torahlifeministries.org/
        messianic/.

"Quick Q&A: Did the Sabbath Change from the Seventh
        Day of the Week to the First?" Quick Q&A: Did the
        Sabbath change from the seventh day of the week

to the first? | The Bible Says That. The Bible Says That.com. Accessed February 2, 2018. https://www.thebiblesaysthat.com/articles/sabbath/quick-qa-did-sabbath-change-seventh-day-week-first.

Roberson, Dianne. "What Is The Hebrew Roots Movement?" churchwatchcentral.com, September 23, 2016. https://churchwatchcentral.com/2016/09/23/what-is-the-hebrew-roots-movement/.

Robertson, David. "Inaccurate Church Traditions: Sunday Sabbath." The Moderate Voice, August 14, 2020. https://themoderatevoice.com/inaccurate-church-traditions-sunday-sabbath/.

Saldarini, Anthony J. "Our Ancient Hebrew Roots." April 2012, April 1, 2012. https://rosemary-bridges.blogspot.com/2012/04/.

Sanchez, Steve. "14. Not to Abolish But to Fulfill (Matthew 5:17-20)." 14. Not to Abolish But to Fulfill (Matthew 5:17-20) | Bible.org. Accessed February 10, 2019. https://bible.org/seriespage/14-not-abolish-fulfill-matthew-517-20.

Schaff, Philip. "The Theological Principles Involved: Import of the Controversy Note 1." Essay. In *History of the Christian Church: Volume 3: Nicene and Post-Nicene Christianity*, 380–80. Broken Arrow, OK: Vision for Maximum Impact, 2017.

"Septuagint." Wikipedia. Wikimedia Foundation. Accessed June 5, 2020. https://en.wikipedia.org/wiki/Septuagint.

Stern, David H. "Chapter 15." Essay. In *Jewish New Testament Commentary: a Companion Volume to the Jewish New Testament*, 274. Clarksville, MD: Jewish New Testament Publications, 1999.

Stern, David. "Misuses of the Torah." kifakz.github.io. Accessed March 18, 2019. https://kifakz.github.io/eng/bible/stern/stern_1-timofeiu_01.html.

Storms, Sam. "The Kingdom of God: Now and Not Yet." Essay. In *Kingdom Come: the Amillennial Alternative*, 264. Fearn, Scotland: Christian Focus Publications Ltd, 2013.

"Tanach (Jewish Bible)." BJE. Board of Jewish Education, August 26, 2020. https://bje.org.au/knowledge-centre/jewish-texts/tanach/.

Telchin, Stan. Essay. In *"Messianic Judaism Is Not Christianity": a Loving Warning to Believers*, 83. Grand Rapid, MI, MI: Chosen, 2004.

Telchin, Stan. *Messianic Judaism Is Not Christianity: a Loving Call to Unity*. Grand Rapids, MI: Chosen Books, 2004.

Tertullian. "Did the First Christian Believers Keep the Sabbath and If so on Which Day?" Christianity Stack Exchange. De Fuga in Persecutione, XIV, October 1, 1960. https://christianity.stackexchange.com/questions/5333/did-the-first-christian-believers-keep-th.

Trimm, James Scott. "In the Defense of the Book of Hebrews." Nazarene Judaism, June 22, 2008. https://nazarenejudaism.com/?page_id=141.

"We Don't Need Teachers Addressing Misusage of Scripture in the Hebrew Roots Movement Part 1." churchword.org, February 26, 2016. http://churchword.org/2016/03/02/dont-need-teachers-addressing-misusage-scripture-hrm-pt-3/.

"What Is the Hebrew Roots Movement." GotQuestions.org. Accessed March 18, 2018. www.gotquestions?.org.

Wilson, Marvin R. "The Root and Branches." In *Our Father Abraham: Jewish Roots of the Christian Faith*, 9–10. Grand Rapids, MI: Wm. B. Eerdmans Publishing, 1989.

Wright, Christopher J. Introduction. In *Knowing Jesus Through the Old Testament: Rediscovering the Roots of Our Faith*, 1. Marshall Pickering, 1992.

FREE FOR THE TAKING

Thank you for purchasing *Shadows and Substance: The Truth About Hebrew Roots and Christian Believers.*

In appreciation, I invite you to download three special E-Books that complement major themes and topics in the book.

- How Should We Celebrate the Feasts?
- Gospel 101
- Don't Let Legalism Rip You Off

To receive all three E-books *free*, go to neilsilverberg.com. Click on the tab: Bought the Book.

Visit www.neilsilverberg.com to learn more about Neil's ministry, books, and teaching series.

You can also subscribe to Neil's Free Podcasts available on iTunes and Spotify.

BOOKS BY NEIL SILVERBERG

Neil is a gifted teacher with a deep knowledge of Scripture whose teaching gift has helped many to see Jesus come alive in the Scriptures. Since the first day God called Neil, he sought to imitate the example of Apollos, who was *"mighty in the Scriptures"* (Acts 18:24). For over forty years, he has diligently given himself to the careful study of God's Word, which has allowed him to gain a life of rich insights into the Scriptures.

Neil's recorded teachings continue to be in demand. He is the author of five books, including *For Truth's Sake: Restoring a Passion for Truth to the People of God*, a book detailing the loss of biblical authority in the Church and how to restore it, and *From the Fold to the Flock*, an exposition of the Parable of the Good Shepherd as providing a basis for the vital contribution of small group ministry. His last book, *New Covenant Life,* explores the riches of the New Covenant, challenging believers to embrace its radical message of grace. He continues to write books, blog, and record new teaching.

Visit www.neilsilverberg.com to learn more about Neil's ministry, books, and teaching series. You can also subscribe to Neil's Free Podcasts available on iTunes and Spotify.